Listening to the Animals

WORKING PARTNERS

A GUIDEPOSTS BOOK

ACKNOWLEDGMENTS

Every attempt has been made to credit the sources of copyrighted material used in this book. If any such acknowledgment has been inadvertently omitted or miscredited, receipt of such information would be appreciated.

All material that originally appeared in *Guideposts* magazine or *Daily Guideposts* is reprinted with permission. Copyright © 1987, 1988, 1993, 1995.

"Real-Life Lassies," by Tony Farrell, is from *Cats & Dogs,* December 1998.

"One Great Sniffer" and "Lassie—a.k.a. Pal" are from *Dog Heroes,* by Tim Jones, Christine Ummel and Jon Van Zyle. Text copyright © 1995 Tim Jones. Published by Epicenter Press.

"The Pack Rat," by Dr. V. R. Howie, "He Found Me!" and "You Can Count on Shep," by Norman Garlick, D.V.M., and "No Ducks for Duke," by R. G. MacKintosh, D.V.M., are from *50 Smart Dogs,* by Dr. Rex Puterbaugh. Copyright © 1999 Rex Puterbaugh. Published by Birch Lane Press.

"Rough Stuff," by Catherine Dold, is from *Smithsonian,* August 1997.

"Avalanche!" is from *Dogs on the Case,* by Patricia Curtis. Text copyright © 1989 by Patricia Curtis. Published by E. P. Dutton.

"Search-and-Rescue Mom" is condensed from *So That Others May Live,* by Hank Whittemore and Caroline Hebard. Copyright © 1995 by Hank Whittemore and Caroline Hebard. Published by Bantam Books, a Division of Bantam Doubleday Dell Publishing Group, Inc. The condensed version was published in *Reader's Digest,* March 1996.

"Underwater Retrievers" and "The Nose Knows Best" are from *Super Animals and Their Unusual Careers,* by Virginia Phelps Clemens. Copyright © 1979 Virginia Phelps Clemens. Published by The Westminster Press.

"The Horse Nobody Knew" is from *Animal Miracles,* by Brad Steiger and Sherry Hansen Steiger. Copyright © 1999 by Brad Steiger and Sherry Hansen Steiger. Published by Adams Media Corporation.

"Humphrey Finds Room at the Inn," by Alison Netsel, is from *Cats & Kittens,* September 1999.

"Brown Dog," by Gene Hill, is from *Field & Stream,* January 1999.

"Like Boys in Autumn" is from *The Rufus Chronicle,* by C. W. Gusewelle. Copyright © 1996 by C. W. Gusewelle. Published by The Ballantine Publishing Group.

"Somewhere Yonder," by Lisa Price, is from *Runner's World,* January 1998.

"Horses on Patrol," by Jenny Wohlfarth is from *Petlife,* July/August 1999.

"Devil Dog," by PFC Peter A. Voss, USMC, is from *Dog & Kennel,* October 1999.

"A Dog Named Silk," by Donald McCaig, is from *Dog World,* August 1999.

(continued on page 208)

Designed by SMS Typography
Illustrations by Michelle Lester
Jacket designed by Dennis Arnold
Printed in the United States of America

Contents

SHARING OUR CHORES

SPECIAL CARE

SUPER SLEUTHS

IN THE SPOTLIGHT

Introduction

My neighbors, the Haas family, live across the road from me on a small farm. In a pasture in front of their house, you can see four horses grazing peacefully when the weather is good. Two of them are handsome and the other two are older and slightly sway-backed. The two beauties are boarded by people who like to ride them in the neighboring fields on weekends. But the other two—well, as Mel Haas puts it, "They helped me put food on my family's table. They've got a place here for life." What Mel means is that when he and his wife bought the farm years ago, the two horses made it possible for him to plant and harvest his crops. They pulled his plow. Now Mel uses a powerful tractor, but he doesn't forget how much his horses helped him in those early years. "Best workers I ever knew," he says.

Animals have been working alongside people since the beginning of time. They enabled us to travel and settle in new places. They made it possible for us to raise our food and then they carried it to market. They went to war when we did and often gave their lives to protect us. They guarded our families, carried our messages, guided us through storms, and when we had a little spare time they entertained us.

They have not been replaced by machines and technology. Instead, animals have been liberated to work with us in new ways. Today they serve as eyes, ears and legs for the disabled. They rescue us when disaster strikes. They protect us by searching out lawbreakers. They find us when we lose our way. They comfort us when we suffer pain and loss. At times they can communicate with us when no one else can. They guard our herds, our homes and our businesses. And they still entertain us.

The true stories in *Working Partners* pay tribute to the animals whose special talents make our lives better. In the most touching words they describe the devotion and love we feel when we and our animals strive together to achieve the impossible.

In FINDING THE LOST, Tim Jones introduces us to Winston, a big yellow Labrador retriever who could find hidden drugs no matter how cleverly they were concealed. Another dog named Thunder specializes in finding people lost in disasters such as earthquakes and the Oklahoma City bombing. Orient, a Seeing-Eye Dog, helps his blind owner, Bill Irwin, find his way along the Appalachian Trail, a journey that takes many months. Not to be outdone, some specially trained dolphins working for the U.S. Navy locate underwater bombs.

The animals in SHARING OUR CHORES take on a variety of jobs. Humphrey, a cat, helps his owners manage a country inn, and Rufus, although only a pup, demonstrates the kind of skill it takes to be a good bird dog. Jenny Wohlfarth reminds us that horses still have a place in the city in her story, "Horses on Patrol," and in "Devil Dog" we meet Chopper III, a rascally Marine who travels with the band. One of the most poignant stories is Donald McCaig's "A Dog Named Silk," the true tale of a border collie who had trouble finding a permanent home. In "The Language of Horses" Monty Roberts helps show horses overcome some behavior problems that keep them from doing their best.

The animals in SPECIAL CARE help us to turn our defeats into victories. You'll meet Jocko, seemingly a loser until a woman with a special need finds him at a shelter and works with him to become an exceptional service dog for the handicapped. Donna Boetig tells us about Flopsy, a funny-looking rabbit who convinces sick kids that looking different is okay. Penny Bargo, on the other hand, has to find some special care for two deaf puppies—and she does. "Feathered Friend," by Jo Coudert, is a most unusual story about an aging woman and a parrot who gives her reason to live.

SUPER SLEUTHS puts us in touch with animals who protect us from harm and wrongdoing. Bruno, a large German Shepherd, has exceptional tracking skills and likes nothing better than finding the "bad guys" who try to run away from his police officer partner. Dan Neil tells us about Ned, a junkyard dog, who will win your heart as he guards his owner's property and supervises a team of puppy assistants. And you will hold your breath as Ebony, a K-9 dog with the American forces in Vietnam, teaches his rookie handler how to find the enemy before he finds you.

IN THE SPOTLIGHT gives our animal friends a chance to steal the show. We meet some of the great ones in the world of entertainment: Lassie (who flunked as a show dog before someone recognized her true talents), Man O'War, the legendary racehorse, Gilmore, a lion cub who became the darling of the advertising world, and a bear who almost broke out of a zoo.

Working Partners gives us an opportunity to see animals as more than pets and companions, as great as those characteristics are. As we become more aware of their incredible talents and skills, we can't help but thank God for their presence and participation in our lives.

PHYLLIS HOBE

WORKING PARTNERS

FINDING THE LOST

"Yes, heroes come in all shapes and
sizes. They gallop and swim and fly.
They snort and whinny and bark. . . ."

ALLAN ZULLO

*I*t happens without warning. Disaster strikes or someone loses his way and there is very little hope for survival. Our high-tech marvels can't help us, and so we turn to the animals, remembering that they have always been ready to put their keen senses to work for us. It's almost as if God created them with these special abilities, knowing that someday we might need them.

Almost? Or certainly?

Real-Life Lassies

TONY FARRELL

$\mathcal{L}$ook into the dark brown eyes of a black Labrador retriever named Thunder, and you'll find the usual love and loyalty of a canine companion. But look a bit deeper, and you might notice something more, for those eyes hold a wealth of experience most family dogs will never know. Far from home and often working in the toughest conditions, Thunder has seen tragedy wrought by the strength of wind, water, fire, and even hate. Thunder's eyes are the eyes of a hero.

Thunder is one of an ever-increasing number of "disaster search dogs" trained to locate victims of calamities—both natural and manmade—wherever they strike. Working in tandem with their skilled handlers, canines like Thunder are quickly becoming indispensable to search-and-rescue teams across the country, ready at the beep of a pager to rush to the scene of the latest catastrophe.

Rescue dogs have served mankind down through the ages, scouting out injured soldiers in wartime and tracking lost skiers, the traditional whiskey kegs bound to their collars. But it wasn't until 1989, in the aftermath of two natural disasters, Hurricane Hugo and the Loma Prieta, California, earthquake, that the Federal Emergency Management Agency (FEMA) began to truly tap the potential of these furry heroes. It's then that "canine search specialists" and their dogs became an essential part of first-strike rescue capabilities, says David Webb, program specialist in FEMA's Urban Search and Rescue Center.

Today, there are 27 FEMA Urban Search and Rescue task forces spread across the nation (8 in California alone). These task forces rely on a network of canine search specialists, as well as paramedics, firefighters, and other emergency personnel, to respond in times of crisis (including homicide cases and rescues). Every locally sponsored, 62-member FEMA task force ideally includes four dog-and-handler teams that must be ready to ship out to a disaster site within 6 short hours of first alert.

In recent years, FEMA disaster dogs have helped locate survivors and deceased victims in the aftermath of Hurricane Fran, the El Niño-wrought mudslides on the California coast, and the earthquake-spurred collapse of a Northridge, California, apartment complex. But it was perhaps the April 19, 1995, bombing of the Alfred P. Murrah Federal Building in Oklahoma City that put both disaster dogs and their handlers to the most trying test. Within hours of the explosion, FEMA dispatched canine search specialists from across the country to Oklahoma City to help locate the scores of bombing victims.

Climbing on precarious piles of rubble. Squeezing through tunnels created by fallen debris. Searching out victims, often deceased. These are scenes from a day in the life of a rescue dog. Which is why the training, temperament, and commitment of both dog and handler must meet strict FEMA standards before the agency will call upon a team to help at a disaster site.

To qualify for the work, disaster dogs must pass rigorous tests designed to measure skill and dedication in often chaotic disaster situations. Candidate canines must demonstrate flawless skills in obedience, agility, and directional control by handlers. Above all, the dog must be able to bark continuously when he happens on a "live find." It's this bark that leads rescue workers to the victim.

Handlers themselves need to train in first aid, rescue-operation techniques, and even basic meteorology, since temperature and humidity affect air movement, which is crucial to "air-scenting," or tracking victims' scent in the air. What's more, canine search specialists operate largely on a volunteer basis, and often they must bear the costs of raising, training, and evaluating their canine charges—costs that can easily run to thousands of dollars a year.

Of course, the intense training required of both members of a canine team has its rewards—among them a strong dog-to-handler bond, sharpened rescue skills, and an ability for the team to "read" each other nonverbally.

It's no surprise to hunters and trackers that the most valuable asset on a disaster dog is his nose. While a human nose has approximately 5 million cells to detect scent, the average dog's nose possesses an estimated 125 to 220 million.

To find a person via "air scent," a dog focuses on body odor—a gas given off by a combination of natural bacteria and the more than 40,000 dead skin cells shed by the human body every minute. Particles of this gas can float on air currents over great distances, through cracks, crevices, and even water. With painstaking training, the disaster canine learns to sniff out these traveling microscopic particles and quickly target the source—the disaster victim.

Ideally, a dog begins training for air-scenting disaster work from the time her handler brings her home as a puppy. Though many different breeds are used in disaster search work, many handlers agree that Labradors and other purebred dogs—especially dogs bred to hunt or to herd—make the best disaster canines, says Michelle Eldridge, a canine search specialist.

Handlers also look for pups who are outgoing, curious, playful, and nonaggressive around humans and animals. And since the handler-dog bond is so important, they seek dogs with whom they have a "connection."

The right dog. The right skills. The right handler. It's all put to the test when the pager beeps with a disaster call. "This is where your training all comes together," says Bob Sessions, Thunder's handler and a reserve member of FEMA's Montgomery County, Maryland, Task Force 1.

Beginning downwind of a specific search sector (so the dogs can better catch the scent of victims), the canines often work out of sight of their handlers and without collars or leashes that might catch on disaster debris. They squeeze through crevices, paw through rubble, and leap gingerly through the smashed remains of buildings. Once a disaster dog locates a survivor, she's trained to bark for as long as it takes rescue personnel to locate her and the victim.

Every disaster requires a different approach from the canine teams. When a hurricane is predicted to strike a U.S. coastal region, for example, search-and-rescue teams often try to arrive before the storm hits to survey potential damage areas. And sometimes Mother Nature adds her own special complications to the work of the canine teams. When a January 1994 earthquake in California caused the Northridge Meadows apartment complex to collapse, canine search specialist Walt Harrison and his dog Misty found themselves riding out more than 100 aftershocks deep within the crevices of the building's pancaked floors.

Yet many handlers agree that the Oklahoma City bombing put canine specialists under the greatest physical and emotional stress in recent years. There, Sessions and Thunder, along with more than two dozen other canine teams, worked tirelessly day after day, often 14 hours and more at a stretch, in the grim search for those who did not survive.

Sessions recalls working hard to keep his emotions at bay to reduce the risk of "telegraphing" his feelings to Thunder—a real and constant concern for canine handlers. "If the handler seems happy, the dog is happy," says Sessions. "If the handler becomes depressed, the dog reads that immediately and loses focus, loses interest, loses drive."

In the wake of the Oklahoma City disaster, families poured out gratitude, local children rushed to meet the dogs and handlers, and letters of thanks arrived on the specialists' bunks, often addressed merely to "The Rescue Dog."

For Bob Sessions, the emotional moment of truth came a year after the bombing, when he and Thunder traveled back to Oklahoma City to attend a memorial service honoring the 169 people killed in the explosion. Once more, near the quiet space where the Murrah building had stood, the people of the city praised the rescue workers, canine search specialists, and disaster dogs who'd come to their aid that terrible day. Two of the heroes—Sessions and Thunder—seemed to share two emotions: Gratitude and peace.

from CATS & DOGS

One Great Sniffer

TIM JONES

$\mathcal{A}$s dog heroes go, Winston Simmerdown almost didn't make it.

A pedigreed yellow Labrador retriever, Winston's line could be traced back six generations. At birth he showed all the promise of a show dog. However, Winston's first two owners gave up on him after he tore up furniture and gardens, clothes and shoes. He was passed on to field trainers, who tried to make him into a hunting dog. Their harsh training tactics took a lively dog and made him depressed and listless. Eventually Winston wound up at what might have been the kennel of last resort.

At that kennel, trainer Tony Bairos saw a dog who was energetic but distrustful and overemotional, who would throw himself against the chain-link fence of his kennel when he was upset. At first Bairos thought Winston might only be good for stud, but he gave the dog one more chance. Experienced at training dogs to find contraband drugs, Bairos started working with Winston. Before any drug-sniffing could begin, he had to gain the dog's confidence. After hours of walking and playing with the dog, the trainer taught Winston to retrieve a rolled-up towel. Over time, he added the scent of first marijuana, then other drugs, to the towel. Winston's reward for finding the

towel was a game of tug-of-war with a section of fire hose—
about the only thing the dog couldn't tear apart. As their work
progressed, Bairos hid the towel in more and more difficult
places until he was sure Winston was ready to work with narcotics officers.

About the time Winston reached the peak of his training, a
citizen's group in Orange County, California, joined the sheriff's
office in the war on drugs by purchasing Winston and paying for
his training. The dog was paired up with Don Lambert, a fifteen-
year veteran of police work. Because of his attachment to
Bairos, it took Winston some time to accept Lambert as his
new partner. But once they formed a bond and completed a
drug-detection course together, Winston and Lambert became
one of the most effective weapons against drug traffic that
Southern California would ever see.

Over their nine-year partnership from 1982 to 1990, Winston
and Lambert accounted for the prosecution of some 1,300 people involved in the drug trade. One judge said of Winston: "He
has more credibility with me than most of the witnesses that
appear before me."

In 1982 the idea of drug-sniffing dogs was relatively new.
Only two other dogs were reported working in California at the
time. As the use of dogs grew, drug dealers took to disguising
the scent of their stashes with coffee, pepper, mothballs, garlic,
even Vicks Vaporub.

It was no use. Winston couldn't be fooled. In one noted
case, Lambert took Winston into a suspect house to search for
drugs. The dealers had scattered mothballs throughout the
house and even packed their drugs in a sealed, cedar-lined
footlocker. Despite all the masking odors, Winston alerted on
the footlocker within minutes. Inside, the police found 4,000

pounds of cocaine and $2.8 million in cash. At another time, Winston detected two pounds of cocaine that had been sealed in Mason jars, then hidden in a strongbox, which was taped above the rear axle of a car. Throughout his career, Winston also found drugs hidden in briefcases, cars, scuba tanks, aerosol cans, and all kinds of secret compartments in cars, homes, and boats.

Winston also could find money handled by drug dealers. Apparently American paper money absorbs odors from the fingers of people who touch it. So if someone has contact with drugs, the money they touch also will carry the scent of the drugs. In the largest bust to Winston's credit, local and federal agents raided a hotel room in Anaheim, California. Winston was brought in to help them search. He quickly led the agents to suitcases and boxes that contained more than $4 million in drug money.

Though it wasn't part of his job description, in one incident Winston saved his partner from serious injury, if not death. While Lambert and Winston worked their part of a drug bust in a parking lot, agents burst into a condominium nearby. A large man dove through a window from the second story and landed on a patio. He charged Lambert, throwing a punch as he came. Lambert ducked. Before he could recover, Winston had driven his full ninety pounds into the man's chest, knocking him to the ground and sinking his teeth into a leg.

Winston's talents went beyond sniffing out drugs and money. As his fame grew, he became a lecturer of sorts, visiting school classrooms with Lambert and carrying the anti-drug message. As Lambert told schoolchildren about the dangers of drug use, Winston demonstrated his abilities and helped to excite the children about the fight against drug traffic.

Winston wasn't only famous with children. Criminals knew about him, too. Police learned that several drug traffickers put a price on Winston's head, one of them for $50,000.

In his nine-year career, Winston was credited with finding more than $44 million worth of illegal drugs and another $34.5 million in drug-related cash, bringing the cash value of his contribution to the fight against drugs to almost $80 million. On top of that, Winston helped police seize the property of convicted drug dealers, including cars, houses, boats, and other possessions worth another $8 million . . . all because of a dog who almost didn't make it.

from DOG HEROES

Walking By Faith

BILL IRWIN

$\mathcal{T}$he March day in 1990 when my Seeing Eye dog Orient, a brown and black shepherd, and I struck out on the Appalachian Trail, it rained buckets. My friend Marvin had dropped us off on a woodland road near the trailhead on Springer Mountain, Georgia. As I stood shivering and drenched, I was suddenly overwhelmed by the prospect of hiking some two thousand miles to Maine . . . blind.

The previous fall I had attended a seminar on "Thru-hiking" the Appalachian Trail. I had decided to be the first blind person to walk the Trail in its entirety, relying not on sight but on faith, and my beloved guide dog. Now, as the sound of Marvin's truck faded down the mountain, I gripped Orient's harness and announced somewhat shakily, "Forward." But I had no idea which way we were going. I had no compass and did not have the advantage of the sun. All I had was God and Orient.

Suddenly, Orient's pace quickened and without any prompting from me, he turned left. It was strange, but what choice did I have but to follow my dog? Soon I realized we were off the woodland road and on a footpath of some sort. Tree limbs began to sweep by my shoulders and legs. The rain thickened. Hours passed and not another soul appeared.

Forty-eight inches of rain and three days passed with my

asking myself over and over, "Where am I?" I had no idea if we were even on the Trail or just going in circles. Each step brought me closer to despair.

Finally, on the third afternoon, I heard voices up ahead—a man and a woman. When I reached them I practically shouted the question, "Where am I?"

"On the Appalachian Trail near Woody Gap, headed north," the woman explained.

We were on the Trail headed north! I nearly broke into a run.

That night, curled in my sleeping bag, I thought about the first three days out. Suddenly I realized that they had not really been much different than any other day in my life. Each day on this unseen path would be a test of faith. And wasn't that what each day of my life amounted to anyway? A test of faith? It would take me eight months to make it to Maine, and each day would be a test.

The Pack Rat

DR. V. R. HOWIE

Jadxia was just a puppy when Amelia bought her while performing at the Ohio Renaissance Festival. The puppy had been named for the Star Trek character, Jadxia Dax. She was half German shepherd and half husky, but you might have thought she was also half pack rat. Since she'd come to Nebraska, she would bring everything imaginable to Amelia—ice chunks from the cattle's watering troughs, dried cow patties, and corn stalks, among other things. If Amelia wasn't available, Jadxia would put her findings in her doghouse. One time, Amelia unloaded groceries from the car and found only one can of orange juice in the bag, whereas she'd been charged for two. The next day, she found the undamaged can of juice in Jadxia's house. Then there was the time Amelia heard a terrible racket outside, and went out to discover Jadxia trying to get a deer—head, antlers, and all—into her house, perhaps as a wall decoration to put above the fireplace in her den?

Amelia's brother, Dan, had driven out from Minnesota to spend one Thanksgiving weekend, and they had had a wonderful day of horseback riding. As they charged down the steep embankment and headed for home at the end of the day, Dan's glasses suddenly flew from his face. Kerry, Amelia, and Dan all dismounted to find the glasses. Hand in hand, they traversed up and down the hill, searching for nearly an hour but to no avail. It was getting cold and dark, so they decided that if they didn't find the glasses on the next pass, they would just have to forget them. But Dan really needed them to see for his drive back to Minnesota. In frustration, Amelia turned to Jadxia and chastised, "You always bring me all this useless junk, why don't you bring me Dan's glasses?" Failing to find the glasses, they returned to the horses for the ride home. As they were preparing to mount up, Amelia called for Jadxia, who came bounding through the tall grass with Dan's glasses held gently in her mouth.

from 50 SMART DOGS

Rough Stuff

CATHERINE DOLD

---

*E*lbow by elbow, like a tiny marine, Tasha is crawling across the dirt. Her task is simple: slither under a pickup truck on the driver's side, crawl out on the passenger side. She's made it halfway, guided by the enthusiastic calls of her owner, Sue Purvis, who is squatting in the dirt near the passenger door. Underneath the axle, though, the black Labrador puppy pauses, looks around and abandons her mission, scrambling instead toward the tailpipe and out into the sunshine. Purvis quickly hustles her back to the driver's side, and again gives her the command: "Go through!" Tasha drops to her elbows. Purvis runs around the truck, shouting encouragement. "Come on, Tasha! Let's go, girl!" This time, Tasha crawls straight across, causing her owner to explode in praise. Thrilled to have made Purvis so happy, Tasha wriggles the entire back half of her body in delight.

Tasha's teammates soon follow: Jazz, an Australian shepherd; Ranger, a chocolate Lab; and Odie, a mixed breed, each do a flawless truck crawl. Amid hugs, praise, high fives and wagging tails, the dogs and their owners then move on to other events in this doggy Olympics being held just outside Dinosaur National Monument in northwest Colorado. One by one, the dogs politely walk on leash while a human at the other end carries an egg in a spoon. They sit patiently in a beached, rocking canoe while the crazy humans jump in and out. And in a new twist on the wet T-shirt contest, each dog dashes under a large tarp with its owner and, after a flurry of flying canvas and wagging behinds, emerges triumphantly wearing a large, drooly T-shirt that moments earlier had been on the human.

Two dozen onlookers alternately cheer wildly and try to trip up the competition. But Tasha's team proves unbeatable. They trounce three other teams, sending both the dogs and their human handlers into a frenzy that rivals the excitement of the real Olympics.

The games are just one portion of an entire weekend of canine fun. Tasha is also enjoying hikes through the scrubby Colorado desert, sleeping under the stars and mingling with more than a dozen dogs from around the state. How much more fun can a 9-month-old pup have? What Tasha doesn't know, though, is that all her activities have been designed with a deadly serious goal in mind.

Like most of the dogs here, Tasha, Odie and Ranger are search and rescue dogs in training. Soon, these prancing pups will be expected to leave their fireside napping spots at a moment's notice and use their noses to find lost children and adults, track down dead bodies and locate people buried under avalanches or concrete and debris.

Sue Purvis and the other dog handlers know that people will expect a lot from their pets. Some will expect miracles. Sheriffs and tearful parents will count on them to do a job that otherwise could require dozens of people and many, many hours of work. So they have come to this remote corner of Colorado for a training weekend sponsored by Search and Rescue Dogs of Colorado (SARDOC). The humans are practicing moving through the desert guided only by map and compass, the dogs are learning how to track human scent, and both are picking up tricks of the trade from veteran search dogs and their handlers. The session, dubbed a "Confidence Weekend," helps to strengthen the trust between dog and handler, reinforcing the notion that just about anything "Mom" or "Dad" asks the dog to do is OK, whether it's fumbling with a T-shirt in the dark during a practice session or riding a chairlift to the top of a ski slope or being hoisted through the air to a noisy helicopter while on a rescue.

Tasha has been in training since she was a mere 11 weeks old. Yet it will be at least another nine months before she is skilled enough to pass the rigorous tests required to become a SARDOC-certified wilderness search and rescue dog. And that is only the beginning. "Wilderness certification is like graduating from high school, the stepping-off point to the rest of the world," explains Wendy Wampler, who owns Jazz. Purvis and Tasha will need to continually practice finding volunteer victims, to be ready to go to work day or night. They might also get specialized training for water or avalanche rescues, cadaver searches and certification by the Federal Emergency Management Agency as an urban disaster search team, the hardest specialty of all.

With lots of practice, Purvis and Tasha might someday be as good at finding lost people as are Wampler and Jazz, who have found numerous individuals in their years of search work. Wampler's favorite rescue, she says, was the time she and Jazz found a 12-year-old girl named Kendra and her dog, who were lost in the mountains near Aspen. While camping with her family, Kendra and her dog failed to return from a solo late-afternoon hike. Searchers from the sheriff's department and other campers were unable to find her, and Wampler and Jazz had been called in at about 3 A.M. Starting at the point where Kendra was last seen, Jazz started following the girl's eight-hour-old trail and, just before dawn, led her handler to the edge of a large field of boulders. "I called out her name again, and this time she responded," recalls Wampler. "I was so relieved." Kendra was cold and wet, but otherwise fine, although she told her rescuers she had panicked earlier and run blindly through the woods, screaming. "But she'd had the presence of mind to keep her dog with her, and she finally sat down and let it keep her warm." Last year, Kendra and her parents came to a dance benefit for SARDOC. In honor of Wampler and her wonderful search dog, they announced, they had named their new puppy Jazz.

Over the Saturday night potluck supper at Dinosaur, the more experienced SARDOC handlers give the newcomers a few tips. Get your dog some earplugs for helicopter rides, they suggest. Always wear cotton so your clothes won't melt in case of fire. They also talk about the traits that can make or break a search dog, including the dreaded "bunny issue." Dogs of all types, from pound mutts to standard poodles, are getting into search work these days, but not all will make the grade. "If your dog chases rabbits and doesn't come right off it when called, you may not have a search dog," warns Kelly Pontbriand, a veteran handler and the coordinator of the weekend's activities. Another handler warns that no matter how much training they receive, some dogs "can't find hamburger in a phone booth." Bunnies and noses aside, many people drop out because they didn't realize that training and maintaining the skills of both dog and handler can require as many as a thousand hours of work a year, no small commitment of time.

Early the next morning, Tasha is preparing to take her first official step toward SARDOC certification—the most basic trailing test, the T1. To get to this point, Purvis and Tasha had started their training with simple hide-and-seek games in the woods near their home in Crested Butte. Tasha, held back by another person, had watched Purvis run off a few times and was encouraged to "go find" her. Once she caught on to that game, she watched one of Purvis' friends run off and found her, then did the same with a stranger. Next, she was faced in the opposite direction while each of those people ran away, forcing her to rely on following the scent left behind. Eventually, to orient Tasha to exactly who she was looking for, Purvis began letting her sniff a scent article, an item of clothing that carries the unique odor of the "victim." Repeated week after week, the training modifies and strengthens Tasha's natural hunting instinct, turning searches into a job that Tasha will readily carry out whenever she is given the command "go find." Her reward, each time she finds her quarry, is a hearty helping of praise and play with a special toy.

"Tasha knows what the routine is now," Purvis says as she straps the puppy into her work harness. Kamala Mirchandani, another handler, is playing victim. She gives Purvis one of her dirty socks (in a plastic bag to prevent contamination by other scents) and walks off into a stand of stunted evergreens while Tasha looks away. When Mirchandani is about 500 feet away and behind a tree, Purvis gives Tasha a quick snoutful of sock and whispers "go find" in her ear. Tasha takes off like a little black rocket, sniffing the ground and homing in on Mirchandani while Purvis and the test evaluators scramble to keep up. In less than a minute, Tasha finds her quarry. She has passed her T1 with flying colors.

Ranger, who is nearly a year old, is doing his first overnight trail at Dinosaur. A howling wind has pushed around the scent trail that was laid last evening, making Ranger's job more difficult, but when owner Darren Weibler gives him the command, Ranger puts his nose to the ground and does his job. Weibler follows close behind. "Good boy, Ranger. Go find her. Go find." Soon Ranger is just a few feet from the victim, who returned to the end of her trail this morning, but because he is relying solely on his nose, he hasn't detected her yet. No one breathes a word or takes a step, for fear of tipping off Ranger. Just as he was taught, Ranger follows the scent on the ground right to the victim, never once using his eyes. His reward: lots of love and a chance to maul his favorite purple monster toy.

Sue Purvis and Darren Weibler and their dogs won't be paid even so much as a bowl of kibble for their work. Yet each has decided to commit a significant amount of time, effort and money to search work. "I've finally found my passion in life," explains Purvis. "Nothing is more thrilling to me. This work combines everything: spending time in the woods, spending time with my dog and concern for people." Wendy Wampler says, "If someone's child is lost, we have to find him. That's what I'd want for my child."

from SMITHSONIAN

Avalanche!

PATRICIA CURTIS

$\mathcal{I}$t was late March in the Sierra Mountains of California when the weather turned ugly. Snow had been falling hard and steadily for several days, building up, and winds gusted at 125 miles an hour. Vehicle accidents blocked mountain roads, ski areas closed down, and some people living on the slopes moved out of their homes.

At a ski area called Alpine Meadows, the highly experienced mountain manager working in the ski patrol office in the summit building was on the telephone and the radio with other authorities in the vicinity, trying to judge the possibility of an avalanche. He sent most of his employees home while he and several of his staff remained on duty.

Anna Conrad, a young woman who lived nearby and worked as a ski lift operator at Alpine Meadows, ignoring the danger, decided to ski from her home to the summit building with her friend Frank. When they arrived, they were soundly bawled out by the mountain manager for the extremely foolish thing they had done. That stern lecture was the last human voice Anna was to hear for a long time.

A few minutes later, Anna was in the locker room when an avalanche tore loose from the top of the mountain. Giant slabs of snow thundered down with a powerful, screaming wind, burying everything in their path. Buildings at the ski area were blasted into the air. Under the force of the first shock wave, the summit building exploded, hurling occupants through the walls or under debris, many to their deaths.

Anna Conrad was thrown to the floor, unconscious. When she came to, she realized she was lying in a small space formed by a row of heavy wooden lockers that had fallen across a bench above her.

It was two hours before rescue teams and equipment, brought in by helicopters, snowmobiles, and tracked vehicles called snowcats, could begin to converge on the disaster site. Wreckage was spread over five acres of the mountain. The sheriff called for search dogs; two dogs and their handlers from a search-and-rescue outfit called WOOF responded.

The dogs, floundering through the huge snowdrifts and debris, eagerly alerted at several spots where equipment and other articles bearing human scent were found, as well as at spots where bodies were later uncovered. Searchers tried using probes—aluminum poles twelve to fifteen feet long—without success. Probes are widely used in searches for victims buried in snow. If a probe hits something soft like a body or a backpack, searchers know where to dig. But snow was still falling fast, and as darkness closed in, threat of a new avalanche sent all the rescuers out of the area.

In her tomb fifteen feet beneath the surface, Anna ate snow and put on layers of clothes that she was able to reach in the lockers that had fallen across her.

The next day, risking their own lives, ski patrols used explosives to control further avalanche slides, and got out of the area just ahead of another storm. For several days, whenever there was a break in the weather, searchers returned and worked frantically with dogs and equipment, but repeatedly they were driven off the mountain by fresh blizzards. Bodies were found, including that of Anna's friend Frank, but Anna Conrad and the mountain manager were still missing. One search dog team heard a dog whining in the debris of the summit building, and rescuers uncovered a very frightened but unharmed German shepherd. She had been brought to Alpine Meadows for training and was in the dog room of the summit building when the avalanche hit.

On the third day, a German shepherd named Bridget alerted above Anna's burial place. Anna heard Bridget's handler, Roberta Huber, calling her, and she yelled back, but no one could hear her. Terror seized Anna as she heard footsteps crunching away in the snow, then silence. She had no idea how much time passed after that (later she learned it was two days). She knew she couldn't last much longer.

But Bridget and Roberta came back as soon as the weather cleared again. By now, the search area was contaminated with the many scents of searchers and equipment, but Bridget pawed and whined at the wreckage of the summit building where she had alerted before. Rescuers brought chain saws, shovels, and earth-moving equipment, working carefully so as not to cause more debris to collapse beneath them. They dug a shaft down into the snow and rubble and lowered Bridget down to tell them which direction to dig, left or right. All hands worked feverishly on the unlikely assumption that whoever the dog was alerting to was still alive. But again the weather drove everyone off the mountain.

At last, after five days trapped in her icy tomb, Anna was lifted out, alive and conscious. Bridget licked her face.

An hour later, the body of the mountain manager was

found. Seven people had died at Alpine Meadows. Anna Conrad lost part of both feet, but she was given the rest of her life, thanks in large part to the brave dog from WOOF.

from DOGS ON THE CASE

Search-and-Rescue Mom

HANK WHITTEMORE AND CAROLINE HEBARD

$\mathcal{T}$he phone rang at about nine o'clock Sunday night, March 3, 1985, at Caroline Hebard's home in Bernardsville, N.J. On the line was a park-service dispatcher, assigned to the Appalachian Trail near the Delaware Water Gap.

Seven children were missing in this Pennsylvania wilderness area. They were part of a church group that had gone for an afternoon hike along the trail. By dark, the temperature had plummeted to 18 degrees, and the windchill factor was around three degrees. Wearing only lightweight jackets, the children might not survive the night.

Park-service rangers knew that canine search-and-rescue volunteers such as Caroline, 40, and her German shepherd, Aly, could cover the terrain faster than a dozen men—and could be invaluable in helping to find the children.

A pioneer in the field of volunteer canine search-and-rescue work, Caroline founded in 1988 the U.S. Disaster Response Team, whose volunteers respond to national and international catastrophes. For four years she was also a member of Northeast Search and Rescue, a group of volunteers ready to search for persons anywhere within the United States.

"I've got a search," Caroline called to her husband, Art, offering him a few details as she pulled on a sweater, coveralls, hiking boots and her red search jacket.

Art and their four children were used to these sudden missions. Alastair and Heather, the two little ones, were asleep. Joanne and Andrew, both teen-agers, got last minute instructions from Caroline, in case she was not back by morning.

The sight of Caroline's red jacket was all Aly needed. He started barking, wagging his tail and racing back and forth.

"Aly, *hier*," Caroline said in German to the dog, who was born in Germany. "*Sitz*." Knowing the ritual, Aly sat while she dressed him in an orange vest bearing a white cross and the word RESCUE in black letters.

It was 9:30 p.m. when Caroline and Aly climbed into her four-wheel-drive rescue truck. She turned on the blue emergency light on top and stepped on the gas.

The daughter of a British diplomat, Caroline was by nature a tomboy. As a child, she loved animals, most especially a black-and-tan Airedale named Mike. When Caroline got in trouble, which was often, she crawled into the doghouse with Mike for comfort.

Caroline grew up to be an adventurous and independent woman. When she was 18 years old, her father gave her a car. Caroline learned to take apart the rear-mounted engine and put it back together again before she drove it cross-country on her own.

She went to graduate school at Stanford University in California and earned a master's degree in linguistics. She also met Arthur Hebard, whom she would marry.

Caroline had planned to teach languages but instead devoted herself to rearing her children. As a hobby, she raised and trained dogs. Eventually she felt the need to do something that would offer mental, physical and emotional challenges. A friend suggested search and rescue—and Caroline's double existence began.

Modern search-and-rescue work was in its early stages in 1972 when the Hebards moved to New Jersey. There Caroline joined the American Rescue Dog Association and quickly realized there was no end to the variety and depth of training required. She became increasingly skilled in backpacking over difficult terrain, wilderness survival and cross-country skiing. She learned to rappel steep cliffs with her 90-pound dog harnessed to the same line and balanced on her chest.

Caroline trained Aly to distinguish human scent from all other odors and to follow the airborne scent of human beings, alive or dead, across miles of wilderness. The complex structure of his nose and the large olfactory lobe in his brain gave him a smelling sensitivity more than 100 times greater than that of any human.

"Have Dog, Will Travel" was the Ramapo, N.J., unit's informal slogan, and Caroline and the group's other members responded to calls for help from emergency-management agencies in the region. As their reputation spread, the small East Coast group was also called for missions farther away.

In September 1985 Caroline and Aly were part of a U.S. team sent to Mexico City after scores of buildings collapsed during an earthquake. Thousands of people had been killed, and thousands more remained buried in tangled wreckage.

When Caroline and Aly arrived, the devastated city was a blur of bewildering activity. There was the thunderous sound of bulldozers and jackhammers. The air was filled with thick dust and foul odors. Squads of masked and helmeted rescue workers were swarming over the rubble to find sparks of life. All around, people were pleading: "Find my husband! Find my wife! My brother! My child! Please!"

Among the tenements and industrial buildings that had collapsed was a 15-story garment factory. It was estimated that as many as 900 women may have been trapped inside. Distraught family members had rushed to the site and, lacking heavy equipment, began digging with their fingers. At first they heard cries from inside, but day by day the cries grew softer and, finally, stopped.

Engineers determined that the building was so unstable it endangered surrounding structures. It would have to be demolished. One relative told Caroline that voices had been heard again, but bulldozers were scheduled to level the place in a few hours.

When Caroline and U.S. team members arrived with their dogs, the building was silent. Were they too late?

"It's very dangerous," an engineer warned. "Those ceilings could fall at any moment. Walk softly."

Caroline crawled inside the building behind another searcher. They climbed through the pancaked rubble, Caroline's helmet lamp illuminating huge rats staring at her.

They moved into a large, still partially intact fourth-floor room where other dogs had picked up a live human scent. The room was filled with ancient sewing machines. On the tables were half-finished sodas, sandwiches, and snapshots of husbands and kids.

Aly moved quickly toward one end of the room where the collapsed ceiling had formed a large pile of rubble. Then the dog disappeared inside a small opening between the rubble and an overhang. Caroline got on her knees and crawled after

Aly, inching along on her belly and holding her breath as long as she could to avoid the horrible stench.

At last she saw Aly in the beam of her flashlight. He was whining as he dug at an impenetrable wall of debris. When she approached, he began to bark. He came toward her and grabbed her flashlight—his signal that he'd found someone.

"Good boy," Caroline whispered. She knew this meant there could be survivors trapped behind the debris.

In fact, a woman was found still clinging to life after a week in the wreckage. Dehydrated and unable to cry out, she summoned the strength to endure. Finally, after half a day of cutting and moving debris, a group of firefighters from Spain, assisted by a Watsonville, Calif., paramedic team, freed the woman and, using a crane, lowered her to safety.

For five days the U.S. contingent of canine search-and-rescue groups worked on 68 separate buildings. They helped rescue 22 people and located countless bodies for victims' relatives.

Once home, Caroline was bombarded with the immediate needs of her family—soccer practice, a school dance. It was impossible, Caroline realized, for her children to grasp what she and Aly had just experienced.

A few mornings later her older daughter, Joanne asked, "What was it like in Mexico?"

"Well, it was . . . it was . . . " Caroline was unable to go on. Her eyes filled with tears. Fifteen-year-old Joanne had never seen her mother looking so fragile. She listened as Caroline explained a little about the suffering and death she'd seen. Joanne found the revelations unsettling. What if her mother had been killed? Caroline had always seemed so in command of her emotions. Yet now she was clearly vulnerable.

Still, Caroline was determined to continue her work. Thirteen months later she and Aly were in El Salvador, searching through the rubble left when earthquakes struck San Salvador.

After that, the missions came steadily. One minute Caroline was busy running a household and driving kids around, and the next she'd be in Bridgeport, Conn., where 28 workers were trapped inside a half-completed building that had collapsed. Or in South Carolina, where Hurricane Hugo had terrorized the coast. Or in Armenia in the aftermath of the devastating earthquake of 1988.

Search-and-rescue work was usually filthy and exhausting. It exposed volunteers to devastation and death, and engraved images of suffering on the mind and soul. To do such work, volunteers had to be motivated by a genuine concern for others, since the tangible rewards never compensated for the physical and emotional price.

Then there are moments such as that freezing autumn night on the Appalachian Trail. Caroline and Aly were assigned to one sector of the trail, accompanied by park rangers. Bolting ahead, Aly raised his nose, trying to catch the scent of the missing children. After one hour of trudging past steep cliffs and through black woods strewn with boulders, they began to see footprints. By then Caroline was exhausted and chilled to the bone.

With nightfall the scent of children's warm bodies would have stood out in the cooler environment, and the colder air descending from high ridges would have carried the scent downhill. But by now the children's bodies had to be too cold to keep producing very much scent.

Suddenly Aly rushed toward a spot and started sniffing with gusto. Caroline knew he had picked up human scent. She could see no signs of human passage, but she had complete trust in her dog. An hour later they saw more footprints.

"We've got more tracks," she said.

Minutes later, they came to a road, and Aly broke into a dead run. Scrambling in the dark over rocks and branches, Caroline knew they were on the right track. The command post was notified.

Thirty minutes and a mile farther on, Caroline was wearing down. Then Aly stopped. He wagged his tail with enthusiasm and disappeared around a bend. A minute later he returned with a large stick in his mouth—the signal that meant he had found them.

Caroline broke into a run as Aly jumped with joy beside her. Up ahead was the entire group of seven children, shivering and whimpering as they huddled for warmth. Some appeared dazed; others began to cry with relief. One little girl had hypothermia, but the rest were fine.

Dawn was breaking when Caroline arrived back home. Soon there was breakfast with Art and the children while Aly slept on the floor. Caroline bubbled over as she gave an account of the mission.

"Way to go, Mom!" exclaimed Alastair. "Way to go, Aly!"

Soon they were on their way to work and school. Caroline did a few chores until her body begged for sleep. Before going upstairs for a nap, she knelt down next to Aly. *"Feiner Hund,"* she whispered into his ear. "Good dog."

from READER'S DIGEST

"He Found Me!"

NORMAN GARLICK, D.V.M.

I was in general veterinary practice at Tacoma, Washington, where there was much ship-building activity, and workers were coming in from all over the United States to work in the shipyards. One day, a man came into the hospital reception room carrying a gaunt, medium-sized black dog of mixed spaniel breed. The man had tears in his eyes, and the dog was obviously exhausted. Its paws were a bloody mess, the pads being totally worn off. As the patient was admitted, we began to get the story.

The man and his family had just traveled from Kansas to Tacoma to work in the shipyards. He had reluctantly decided that he would have to leave his dog in Kansas, and had placed him with another family there.

The day he brought the dog to us he had just left work. It was less than a week since he had arrived in Tacoma. As he walked out the gate toward his car, he was met by his dog who he had left in Kansas! He was totally overwhelmed with emotion. He gathered him up in his arms and brought him straight to us to provide the care he would need to recover. There was every reason to believe the man's account—the condition of the dog was consistent with a journey of almost 2,000 miles on foot, most of the way without adequate water, and probably little or no food. The dog made an excellent recovery and was soon restored to his master, this time for life.

from 50 SMART DOGS

Underwater Retrievers

VIRGINIA PHELPS CLEMENS

The United States Navy jet flew steadily on its easterly course. Far below, the whitecaps of Atlantic Ocean waves rolled across the water.

Inside the plane were two bottlenosed aquanauts—two dolphins named Bubbles and Rudy. They lay patiently in slings that hung inside topless wooden crates. The slings, hammock-like stretchers, had openings cut out for the dolphins' flippers.

Hoses controlled by automatic timers periodically sprayed the animals with a fine stream of water to keep their skins from drying out. The dolphins were turned occasionally so their weight was not always pressing on the same side. Bubbles and Rudy didn't really mind being out of water. In fact, they were quite comfortable in their slings.

Bubbles and Rudy were two young, male Atlantic bottle-nosed dolphins. They were being sent to find a live bomb that had fallen off a plane into the Atlantic Ocean off the coast of Spain. The dolphins' job was to locate the bomb so it could be recovered.

After several hours the plane finally touched down at an airport not far from the Spanish coast. Bubbles and Rudy were carried off the plane, and, still in their slings, put into the back of a truck. The drive to the dock, where a boat was waiting for them, wasn't as smooth as the plane ride, but the dolphins just rocked gently in their slings. Dick Hammond, their handler and trainer, sat beside them and sprayed water by hand onto their backs and heads.

"Easy, boys, we'll soon be there," he said soothingly. "Then you'll have some work to do."

Once loaded on the boat, Bubbles and Rudy became a little restless, clicking and whistling to each other. They knew that the ocean was near and their journey would soon be over.

Suddenly the roar of the boat's motors died down to a low rumble and, finally, a purr. Then they stopped. The boat rocked back and forth as the waves passed under and around it.

"O.K., let's get them into the water," Dick called out to the other men.

After attaching the sling that held Bubbles to the boat's crane, the man at the controls carefully hoisted the dolphin up over the side and into the water. Dick was there to help Bubbles wiggle free. Next came Rudy.

"All right, Rudy, just a minute and you'll be on your own, too," Dick said.

As soon as they were loose, the two dolphins skimmed through the waves, leaping high into the air and flopping down to splash Dick as he climbed into a small raft that was tied next to the boat. Their gray, streamlined bodies crisscrossed swiftly underwater as they played with each other.

"O.K., boys, warm up with these," Dick said. He tossed a couple of fish to each dolphin. The animals leaped up and each caught a fish in midair before snatching the ones that had fallen into the water.

After giving them a few more minutes to play, Dick whis-tled to the two dolphins. Obediently, they swam alongside the raft so Dick could put on their harnesses. A magnetic ring placed over each dolphin's beak, or nose, would stick to metal objects. The dolphins had been trained to bring these rings up to the bomb. With a flip of their heads they could toss them off their beaks so the magnetic force would hold them in place on the explosive. Then a small float attached to a line would pop up to the surface. Divers could see the line and follow it back down to the bomb. Grappling equipment could then be attached to bring the bomb up to the surface.

Using hand signals, Dick commanded the dolphins to start the search. Both dolphins hyperventilated, taking several deep breaths to draw more oxygen into their bodies, before diving. Then down they plunged into the ocean's blackness.

Once on the bottom, the dolphins circled and weaved in different directions, searching for the bomb. Making a clicking sound, they moved their heads from side to side so they could pick up any clicks that echoed back from their target. Dolphins use echolocation, a kind of sonar, to find objects. Their eyes are almost useless in the underwater darkness. They send high-frequency sound waves through the water and "read" the vibrations that bounce back to them from various objects.

After more than three minutes, Rudy swam up to the surface. Bubbles followed thirty seconds later. They cruised slowly around the boat, waiting for Dick's next command. Dick threw them each a fish, which they gobbled up eagerly.

"O.K., fellows, let's try it again."

At a wave of Dick's hand, the dolphins again hyperventilated and dove to the ocean bottom. This time, both dolphins appeared between the waves before three minutes had passed. The rings were missing from their beaks, and, as the dolphins whistled and squealed for their reward, two little floats popped up on the crest of a wave about twenty-five yards off to the right of the boat.

"Good boys," said Dick, praising them, as he threw a bucket of fish into the water.

Bubbles and Rudy darted back and forth, gulping down the fish as fast as they could. After circling and leaping, both together and separately for several minutes, the dolphins slowed down and swam calmly side by side around the boat. Their backs slid along just below the surface of the water, while their dorsal fins cut through the waves. Occasionally, one would stop, poke its head out of the water, and whistle to Dick.

"All right, let's go home," Dick said as he signaled to Bubbles to swim into the sling he had ready for him. The human divers had already started their descent to the ocean's bottom. In just minutes, Bubbles and Rudy had saved them hours of work searching for the bomb.

from SUPER ANIMALS AND THEIR UNUSUAL CAREERS

The Horse Nobody Knew

BRAD STEIGER AND SHERRY HANSEN STEIGER

On his ranch, near Billings, Montana, Jeremy was in the fields rounding up the cattle one day when he noticed what appeared to be an old stray horse running in the distance. Jeremy and Ray, his ranch hand, were each on their faithful horses, and they were very familiar with nearby ranchers and the horses they owned.

"That's something us ranchers keep track of the way some neighbors make it a point to know who goes in what car in the neighborhood and of every new car or trade that goes on around them," Jeremy explained later. "Not really snoopy, more like a neighborhood watch kind of thing."

On seeing the horse, both men gave a silent nod and shrug of the shoulders as if to say, "I don't know anyone who owns that horse—never seen that one before." Their own horses suddenly seemed a bit restless, as if they too had picked up on the unknown intruder horse.

The sight of a horse without a rider was pretty rare near their ranch—in fact, it was pretty rare in any part of the county. Jeremy turned to Ray and yelled, "You keep an eye on the cattle while I see if I can't catch up with that ole gray and see what's up."

Off Jeremy went, riding like thunder to catch up with the old gray. It didn't take him very long, since she appeared to be rather old and not in the best of condition. The gray got spooked and took off, with Jeremy chasing her. Finally, the gray seemed to be getting too tired to go much farther. Jeremy called to her, "Come on, Old Gray, let me have a look at ya. I'm not gonna hurt ya. I just need to see where you came from. Someone might be missing you by now."

Jeremy got off his horse and managed to gently reach out to the gray. He started petting and stroking her, trying to calm and reassure her. He looked her over for any sign of branding identification marks. Finding none, he said to her, "Well, Old Gray will be your name, if it already isn't, and I guess you'll just have to come with me until I can check out around town to see if anyone knows about you."

He always carried some extra rope with him, so Jeremy fashioned a lead for the old gray and led her back to where Ray was waiting. "Any marks on her?" Ray asked. Realizing that Ray meant I.D. marks, Jeremy answered, "Not a single one that I can find. Let's take her back with us and give her a little kindness while I check around to see what gives."

After about two weeks, not a single person in town or in the surrounding ranches had any idea where this horse could have come from. So Jeremy was given the go-ahead to keep the mare if he chose.

Jeremy kind of took to Old Gray. Somehow, he felt a close identification with her, since he himself had been raised by an uncle and aunt and had spent several years in an orphanage when they were killed in a crash. In some strange way, he felt a strong kinship with this horse and felt good about being able to clean her up and give her some good nutrition. He provided her with some extra supplements to get her in better health.

"You cleaned up pretty darn good," Jeremy said to Old Gray one day as he gave her her daily brushing and a couple of rubs on the head. "And I have to say, I'm kinda glad nobody came to claim you. You and I are family now, aren't we, Old Gray?" He was fully satisfied that she understood every word. "There are folks around who say I ought to just sell you off for glue. They say you're too old and ragged to be good for anything anymore. But heck, they probably say that about me too, behind my back when I ain't lookin'. Pals, we'll just be pals, and pals is good enough for me."

Several months later, Jeremy volunteered to do some repair work on a neighboring rancher's barn and tend to a few chores while the rancher was away on urgent family business. Jeremy drove over to the place in his old pickup, telling Ray and his wife where he'd be and telling them it would only take him several hours.

When Jeremy had been gone for a little over an hour, Ray heard some odd noises out in the barn. When he got out there, he saw that it was Old Gray acting up. She was snorting, kicking up her heels, butting against the corral, and carrying on something terrible. "What on earth is wrong with you, Gray?" Ray puzzled. The other horses were reacting to Gray's uneasiness, and it looked as if it could become a troublesome situation.

Ray tried to talk to Gray and get close enough to her to see what was spooking her or setting her off. "Are you sick, old girl? What is it?" Ray couldn't get close to Gray, who was bucking wildly. Just then, Gray broke the wooden posts and took off out of the barn, racing as if she had a destination in mind.

Ray yelled for his wife Doreen to come out and help, as he was torn between chasing Gray and keeping the other horses from following suit. His wife was out in a flash and took over in the barn while Ray chased after Gray.

There was no way he could catch up with her. He was back in the barn within ten minutes, completely out of breath and panting. "I didn't know she had that much life in her yet— she's gone! I'm going to hop in the car and see if I can find out where she went."

After driving some of the back roads and not finding Old Gray, Ray thought he'd better go tell Jeremy about the bizarre breakout and the missing Gray right away, since he knew how attached Jeremy had become to her.

As Ray pulled into the long drive that led to the ranch where Jeremy was working, he thought he saw smoke billowing from where the barn would be. He stepped hard on the gas pedal. Sure enough, when he got to the barn, it was on fire— and there was Old Gray!

She was going back and forth into the blazing barn. She led Ray to where Jeremy lay unconscious. It was apparent that Old Gray had attempted to drag Jeremy out of the barn with her teeth, biting onto Jeremy's wrangler jacket. She had Jeremy just about out of the barn when Ray got to him.

It turned out that Jeremy had been in the barn pulling on something that was perched precariously above him, and whatever it was had fallen on him hard enough to knock him out. The source of the fire was still unknown, but it *was* very apparent that in not many more minutes, Jeremy would have been asphyxiated. He owed his very life to this Old Gray he had grown so attached to.

"How she possibly could have known that I was in trouble—or even where I was—is beyond me," Jeremy later said, patting her on the head and hugging her hard. "You and me, we'll always stick together, now, won't we, my Gray Beauty?"

Ray offered Gray some sugar cubes, saying, "Thanks, Gray—you not only saved my pal, but you taught me a good lesson too."

As they left the barn, Ray said, "Jeremy, I sure take it back about the 'good for nothin' but glue' comment I made. I hope you'll accept my humble apologies. That gray is worth more than gold. She's quite a treasure!"

from ANIMAL MIRACLES

Sharing Our Chores

*"Making companions of other species
is one of the very oldest things we do.
Fire is older, chipped stone tools are
older, but almost nothing else is."*

ROGER CARAS

$\mathcal{A}$nimals seem to like nothing better than to help us do something we can't do by ourselves. Call them to your side and they'll come running. Ask them for their strength, intelligence and dedication, and they'll give them gladly. Best of all, let an animal know you depend on him and appreciate his talents, and you've got one happy creature.

Perhaps there's a lesson here for us. Perhaps we're all happier when we're helping each other.

Humphrey Finds Room at the Inn

ALISON NETSEL

The idyllic town of Manchester, Vermont, offers breath-taking panoramas and an array of activities for visitors year-round. During the mild spring and summer months, tourists and locals enjoy fly-fishing in the Battenkill River and bicycling the back roads. As autumn settles in, the sugar maples turn the country-side into a dazzling vista of red and gold. When winter takes over and snow covers the mountains, the nearby Bromley and Stratton ski areas attract novice and expert cross-country and downhill skiers alike.

A town as charming as Manchester wouldn't be complete without a Victorian bed-and-breakfast, and the Manchester Highlands Inn fills the bill admirably. Visitors at the inn sleep peacefully beneath down comforters, and feast on breakfasts that include such items as lemon soufflé pancakes and Vermont cheddar omelets. The inn's proprietors and hosts are Patricia and Robert Eichorn, who, along with a staff of six, strive to make each guest's stay a pleasurable experience.

The Eichorns are aided by Humphrey, the inn's resident cat, who is its symbol of rest and relaxation. Humphrey is a 12-year-old Maine coon cat with a long coat of brown, black, gray and white fur, a bushy tail and large, golden eyes. Humphrey first came to the Eichorns nine years ago by way of a referral to the Bennington County Humane Society from a family that was looking for a home for him.

The Eichorns welcomed Humphrey into the Manchester Highlands Inn, their place of business and their home as well. The inn consists of the main house and the carriage house, both built in 1898. The inn has 15 guest rooms, along with a living room, game room, pub and outdoor swimming pool, all of which encourage the guests to relax, renew and return, as the promotional brochures suggest. The house also features a porch from which a spectacular view can be seen of the sunset over Mount Equinox.

Humphrey, who has been neutered, is allowed outdoors to join the guests. "He loves to sit in the garden and enjoy the view," says Robert Eichorn. Humphrey makes himself equally at home inside the inn, where he can often be found napping on a sofa. If any of the guests are allergic to cats, Humphrey is kept out of the inn's common areas. Guests aren't permitted to bring their own pets to the inn, but Humphrey is allowed into the guests' rooms by invitation, often helping to assuage the feeling of loneliness some people experience over the absence of their own pets.

"He is such a gentle soul," says Patricia Eichorn of Humphrey, "he has never bitten or scratched a guest."

His affectionate nature and love of comfort make Humphrey easy to find. "He loves to jump onto the dining room chairs when guests get up to refill their coffee cups," laughs Patricia Eichorn. "One woman made me take a photo of her sitting across from Humphrey at the breakfast table. Sometimes guests pull up a chair so Humphrey can join them."

It was the Eichorns' love of cooking and entertaining which led them to their current occupation as innkeepers. Before opening the inn, they had both worked for an international airline in various managerial positions. The Eichorns, who are in their early 50s, left Long Island, New York, where they had both grown up, and moved to Vermont to start the inn. They were accompanied by their daughter, Jennifer, now 25, and their son, Christopher, now 21.

Humphrey has become as much of a draw to the inn as the nearby skiing, fly-fishing, canoeing, hiking and biking. The first thing people ask when they arrive is: "Where is Humphrey?" says Robert Eichorn, "especially those who have visited his page on our website. He also gets e-mail from time to time." In fact, the inn's e-mail address is *humphrey@highlandsinn.com*. The website, *www.highlandsinn.com*, features information about Humphrey, the inn and the surrounding area, as well as up-to-the-minute room rates and availability.

"It's love at first sight," says Patricia Eichorn of the guests' reactions when they see Humphrey.

from CATS & KITTENS

Brown Dog

GENE HILL

Lately there's been an upsurge in the popularity of what's called the "versatile gun dog." The term covers several breeds, all European in origin. Now, I'm not disputing any claims of this nature, but I'd like to point out that this country has had such a dog for longer than I can remember. It's not really a breed; it's more of a type. I had one when I was a kid and nearly everyone else I knew had one at some time or another. You might call it a "brown dog."

No farm can be said to be properly run unless there's a brown dog in some position of authority. Brown dogs will herd cows and pigs, keep the chickens out of the garden, and keep the area free from skunks—which accounts, in large measure, for their distinct odor. No small boy can be properly raised without one.

I think it was Robert Benchley who once remarked, "Every boy should have a dog; it teaches him to turn around three times before lying down." Brown dogs do a great deal more than that. They provide a boy with excuses for adventures, teach him how to whistle loud and clear, improve his throwing arm, and, most important, instill in him the incredible responsibility that comes with being loved unquestioningly, totally, and irrevocably.

Brown dogs are famous for their nonchalant, sophisticated attitude. They have an air of having seen it all before. Mine would stop now and then and stare into the middle distance, as if pondering some crucial question. Then, having resolved it to his satisfaction, he'd shake his head as though wishing he could impart the gem of knowledge to me, but somehow feeling that I simply would not understand its value.

A brown dog will tolerate a boy's family but will not get too involved. If the boy is absent, say, during school days, he will curl up close to where the master will first appear on coming home and wait. Even if there are things he has to attend to, rounds to make or whatever, never doubt that the sound of the school bus will fall on his ears first and farthest away.

When the owner of a brown dog I know went off to college, the dog would move out to the end of the lane about a day and a half before his pal was due home. How did he know? I haven't the foggiest idea. Since the boy's father didn't know when to expect him home either, it's even more mysterious—except that as a brown dog, you're expected to know such things and it's your job to act on them.

In general, brown dogs figure out what has to be done and then do it. If you need someone to sit and listen to your problems, they'll lend a most sympathetic ear. If you're bursting with spring, they'll race up and down the brook with you. I suspect they like summer best of all because everyone's home. Brown dogs are very fond of parties: swimming hole picnics, hayrides, summer softball games, fireworks, bicycling, fishing trips, and camping out. They make good outfielders and lifeguards. As a kid, I wouldn't have dreamed of sleeping on the lawn without my brown dog to watch over me; nor would he have allowed it in the first place.

Most problems with brown dogs stem from their intelligence and unswerving desire to please. Mine went along with me and my first .22 when I used it to get rid of a few groundhogs in one of the pastures. I suppose I shot two or three; I forget. But he got the idea that we wanted groundhogs, and nearly every day, all that summer, he brought one home. The problem was that he didn't bring them home immediately, but waited a day or so until they were more impressive—both in size and smell. That little lesson wasn't lost on me, and from then on there were certain outings I went on alone.

I used to think, with pride overflowing, that my brown dog was mine. Now I know better. We never really own a dog as much as he owns us.

Once when I was very small and very sick my mother put my brown dog in bed with me against everyone's advice. "They need each other," she said, and that was that. She understood brown dogs and their peculiar magic.

from FIELD & STREAM

Like Boys in Autumn

C. W. GUSEWELLE

---

*T*eal season in the Midwest arrives oddly out of time. The days still are warm and the leaves have not yet started to color when the early flights of green-wings and blue-wings come racing down the continent to linger a few weeks, then hurry on ahead of the cold.

I was involved with several friends in a duck lease 90 minutes south of the city—a shallow, muddy little pond of 40 or so acres, with two blinds. Some years there was too little water. Other years the creek flooded, overflowed the pond and washed the blinds away.

A few mornings each season, usually just before the freeze, the mallards—the big red-leg flight ducks—came in great numbers and the shooting was fine. Most days we watched them pass over high, looking for larger and more promising water. But it was the early teal opener that began the hunting year, and it was good to be down the road and out before first light, even if it seemed queer to be sitting in a duck blind in shirtsleeves.

Mainly I went out that morning for Rufus's benefit. That's how men often explain their hunting: They only do it out of obligation to the dogs. This time it was the truth.

To accustom him to sudden noise, I'd started by banging his food dish and rattling pans at feeding time. Then we graduated to a cap gun, and from that to blanks from a starter's pistol. The neighbors must have wondered why, with all that shooting, no ambulance ever came to the house.

He was ready now for the racket of some light shotgun loads at close range. So we loaded in the 3 o'clock morning dark, his crate and my chest waders in the back of the station wagon, him beside me on the front seat, and drove to the pond.

The sky was cloudless and full of stars. No one else was out that morning, so we would have the place to ourselves.

The blind was on the far bank, a waist-deep wade of most of a quarter-mile. Briefly I thought of trying to carry him out, Rufus under one arm, gun and bag of decoys in the other. But, loving water as he did, he plunged directly in and dog-paddled cheerfully beside me as we crossed.

The day came on with a rush—sparkling, windless, unpromising for ducks.

"Well, little fellow," I told Rufus, "maybe after while we'll let off a shot or two anyway, just to see how you like it."

I'd hardly said it when there was a whispering rush over the blind as a flight of a dozen green-wings sped in from behind, turned once and dropped on cupped wings straight to the decoys. My first startled shot went wild. The second put a drake in the water.

The surprise was what followed.

Except for songbirds in his yard and in the park, he'd never seen a feathered creature of any sort. But at the sound of the shot and the splash of the teal, Rufus was out of the blind and swimming for the prize.

He towed the duck in by its wing. And his expression,

when I took it from him and lifted him back in with me, was both excited and proud. He sniffed the teal with interest, licked it once. Then, I swear, he looked skyward to see if there might be others coming.

"You're not a duck dog," I told him in a mock-chiding way. "You're a *bird dog*!"

He was not yet 6 months old. And I think it was in that moment that I understood, in a way I really hadn't before, that Providence had given me a very uncommon companion to share my seasons in the field.

On trips to the country as the year turned he did more puppy things: chased grackle flocks, dug up field-mouse burrows, was not above pursuing a rabbit if one presented itself.

At home, he ate a library book and a potted flower. Then ate the flower's pot. He learned to sit atop his doghouse like the beagle in the cartoon, looking in through the kitchen window to be sure his bowl was being filled at the appointed hour.

And yet, from the beginning, he seemed to understand somehow the principal business of his life.

On our early walks, first in the park and then in a nearby patch of city woods, he'd never simply tagged along. He forged ahead, testing the limits as the best and the brightest are wont to do. Then I tied a quail wing to a fishing line and hid it in the grass for him to find.

Immediately, in those evening sessions on the lawn, he put his puppy ways aside. The scent of that wing—a last year's wing, saved over in the deep freeze—spoke a language in which he was born already eloquent. The look then in his golden eyes was remarkable to see.

On a sunny day, unseasonably hot for this month, I'd gone

to the farm on an errand, and Rufus had ridden with me. Business finished, we set out to stretch our legs.

The quail, a solitary rooster, was in an unlikely place, on the face of a rocky slope below the fieldstone foundation of a vanished homestead and the sprouty glades that must once have been that settler's little fields.

Possibly a rabbit, I thought as I walked in behind him, though I couldn't see one. *Or it could be a mouse.* Just under his nose, out of a tuft of weeds no larger than a saucer, the single bird burst up. Unready, I shot late and was lucky to fold him just before he topped the rise.

Rufus brought the bird to me as neatly as if we'd been doing this forever, and I let him mouth the quail a bit before I took it from him. I hugged him, relishing the moment, but he was restless to be off looking for the others. There weren't any others, though. Just the one—the first bird over the first point of his first season.

And there was better, much better, to come.

The wind turned around from the north, hard frost burned the vegetation brown, and those games played with the wing on a city lawn during spring and summer became real on a raw afternoon, in a brushy hedgerow along the crest between two emerald fields of winter wheat.

I was hunting with my longtime friend and newspaper colleague, Fred Kiewit, and two of Fred's regular quail-hunting pals. We'd prospected down an unproductive draw and were bound back up toward the road and the parked car, the wind at our backs, a covey of quail evidently running ahead in the high grass along the quarter-mile of hedge between the wheat fields.

Rufus was well out in front, working a section of the hedge back toward us, against the wind, then looping out and farther on to try a new section. He was smelling where the birds had been. Then where they had been more recently.

Then, finally, *where they were now.*

So intent we were in watching him that the covey, when it exploded just under his nose and ours, flew off all but unmolested.

The others spoke of it afterward—men in their 60s and 70s, old bird men and old dog men. Of how, in quail-hunters' language, he'd *set* the birds and held them. Of the style and steadiness of the point. Surely he wasn't a green pup, they said. Why, they'd seen dogs in their second and third season not work as well.

Rufus was indifferent to this praise. But I went a little giddy, like the father of some halfback who had just gone 70 yards through the Dallas Cowboys defense to win the Super Bowl.

That night I spent most of two hours trimming out cockleburs, hair by hair, from his tender underparts. It was a labor of pure devotion—in gratitude for which, the next day, he hid his dish again and ate another flowerpot. And then sat looking in from the roof of his house with pure devilment and pure puppy in his eyes.

We are not quite grown, yet, either of us. May these autumns of our extended childhoods be very long.

from THE RUFUS CHRONICLE

No Ducks for Dude

R. G. MacKINTOSH, D.V.M.

$\mathcal{A}$n old friend invited me to a duck-hunting club because I had taken care of his Labrador retriever, Dude. This big and overweight dog lay on the floor of the duck blind on his gunny sack, and peered out of a hole facing the pond where the wooden decoys floated gently. The hiss of wings signaled approaching birds. This told me and Dude to be ready. I stood and fired twice as the mallards powered in. They flared up and away, but Dude plunged into the icy water for his retrieve. However, there were no ducks. I am not the world's best wing shot. I gestured to the dog to wait, and it wasn't long until the ducks returned. BANG! BANG! As the ducks flew away I noticed that the dog had gone out of his hole in the blind and stood belly-deep in the water. No plunging retrieve this time; just an observation. Dude looked back at me, walked back into his bed, shook himself, and lay down. I apologized to old Dude, and promised, "next time."

Twenty minutes later, he looked up at me—when we heard the sound of wings. I fired twice. Dude arose and went to his little doorway, looked out, and then lay back down once more. When he looked at me this time, I felt quite humble.

Again I fired and missed. You'd think I would have learned.

Dude had. He opened his eyes from his nap, looked at me, turned over, and went back to sleep.

Do you think dogs can't think? They don't even need to talk.

from 50 SMART DOGS

Somewhere Yonder

LISA PRICE

$\mathcal{W}$e both know the end of our time together approaches, my dog and I, but still we linger. I lay on the floor, my arm around his furry neck, scratching his chest as I watch the women's Olympic marathon.

Watching the marathoners reminds me of all the miles Kliban and I have run together, on the roads and through the years. We have run together for possibly 10,000 miles as I trained for races, through all seasons, and have shared the time between my 23rd and 38th year.

I was there at his birth. And his presence has been the one constant thread, the singular unchanging color in the tapestry of 15 years.

Threads have ended in the tapestry, people have gone, and there are memories that just the two of us share. "He's just a dog. . . . " people who have never had a dog might say. But there is a wisdom, born in the shared years, that glows in those luminous, round brown eyes, now above a graying muzzle and clouded with the blue of old age.

When we hiked the Appalachian Trail together, we fell into a pattern that mirrored the way he lived in my life—his self-appointed guardianship. He always trotted ahead to wait for me, standing protectively where he could scan the trail ahead while still keeping me in sight.

As I slept, he protected, once even charging a wild boar that rooted around our tent in Tennessee.

Twice on the trail he disobeyed. Once, in Virginia, he returned from his vantage point and blocked my path. As I kept trying to go around him, I grew irritated—until I finally heard the ominous shakes of the rattlesnake up ahead.

And in New York, where we had hiked a long two days without water during a drought, he suddenly disappeared for a stretch of minutes. I yelled at him when he finally reappeared and approached, until he rubbed his wet chest against my legs and then led me to the water.

The words "good dog" made him quiver with happiness, and that was all he ever wanted.

But now the arthritic hips have finally failed, the vision has dimmed, and the internal systems have worn out. Still, how I dread the last goodbye, that scene at the veterinarian's office when he will be "put to sleep."

And yet, as I hold him and feel his thin shoulders, I know it is time. So I tell him so and start to cry. Monday, I tell him, I'll make the appointment. You've been so tough and brave, protecting me all your life, it's okay, you can rest now.

"You're a good dog," I tell him, and he responds with a quiver. "It's *me* you've been waiting for, I finally understand. I love you, and I'll never forget you. I wish you could be with me my whole life, but I'm ready, it's okay."

I get up and go in the other room, flick on the computer and try to work for a while, crying and writing.

When I return 20 minutes later, Kliban has gone with dignity and peace, protecting me this one last time.

He is wrapped in a quilt made of T-shirts from the running races he helped me train for, and buried in a shady spot with a view of the mountains. And he is somewhere yonder on the long trail, where he has gone ahead to wait for me.

from RUNNER'S WORLD

You Can Count on Shep

NORMAN GARLICK, D.V.M.

While I was studying veterinary medicine, I had the opportunity to work on a small dairy farm near the town of Eatonville, Washington. The owner had done his own dog training, and Shep, an Australian shepherd dog, was a natural, with highly developed herding instincts.

At this dairy farm, cattle-driving by people on foot was a waste of time, and the cattle could not be relied on to come in for their milking.

Every morning and evening at milking time, Shep would wait at the milk house door, his eyes filled with obvious excitement, and his body tense with anticipation. At the words "Go and get them," spoken by any of the three farmhands, Shep would race out into the pasture, and within twenty to thirty minutes, he had the cows entering the lane leading to the barn. Shep would slip under the fence and race to the end of the lane, where he would watch while the cows came in through the gate. If all the cows came through, Shep would expect some well-deserved praise. However, if one or more of the cows were missing at the gate, Shep would race back into the pasture, and in a short time he would retrieve the missing cows. He never had to go back more than once, and he always knew when every cow had been accounted for. He also knew which of the cows were most likely to hide out. Shep lived for his work and loved it. I only wish that he could have learned to milk those cows and spare me the task!

from 50 SMART DOGS

Horses on Patrol

JENNY WOHLFARTH

We don't expect to see horses trotting down Bourbon Street in New Orleans or shepherding a swarm of school buses in a city like Cincinnati, but they're out there—in cities all across the United States. They don't have badges and don't wear uniforms, but police horses are working the pavement in cities like these every day of the year.

"What we're asking these horses to do is way out of the realm of what is natural to them," explains Officer Jill Schramm of the Cincinnati Mounted Police Unit. "These animals were meant to be out in the middle of a field eating grass, and here we are, riding them into narrow alleys and over manhole covers, asking them to walk through fire and stand still for gunfire, expecting them to remain calm when ambulances, buses and cars speed by. They do this eight hours a day, six days a week. They're pretty amazing."

While the use of horses in police units might seem nostalgic or outdated in today's world, mounted officers claim that nothing outperforms a horse in crowd control and community relations. In addition, urban studies have shown that, compared to police cruisers, police horses are cheaper, more fuel-efficient, more visible, more citizen-friendly and more environmentally sound. Plus they're a heckuva lot easier to park on a crowded city street.

"Sure, you can't make as many radio runs on a horse as you can in a car," Schramm admits, "but when there are a thousand people who need to be moved along, an officer on foot or in a patrol car can wait around until he's blue in the face. But an officer on a horse really has the advantage, using the power of a 1200-pound animal to shuffle the crowd along.

"We have great visual advantages in a crowd when we are on horseback, because we're sitting about nine feet in the air," Schramm continues. "Basically, we can do everything a police officer in a car does—handcuffing or pursuing suspects, writing tickets, restraining suspects—everything. Well, everything except transporting prisoners. There's not much room for that on the back of a saddle."

Lieutenant Tommy Smegal and his fellow officers with the New Orleans Mounted Patrol Unit use their horses to escort troublemakers out of the crowded French Quarter, clear the streets for ambulances, and direct the flow of pedestrian and vehicle traffic. "These horses can have thousands of people milling around them and don't think anything of it," Smegal says. "Bourbon Street from Thursday to Sunday, even when it's not Mardi Gras, is a solid wall of people from 8 at night until 3 in the morning. And these horses make it possible to keep it all under control."

Because of these working conditions, it's obvious why the police horses must be calm and easy-tempered animals that can learn to trust their riders in very unfamiliar situations. Police horses are usually tall—about 16 hands—tall enough to really give the officer good visibility in a crowd. They are always solid-colored, with preference given to browns, bays, blacks, chestnuts and sorrels. Most police units acquire horses through auctions or private donations, and prefer geldings between the ages of 5 and 16, though some hardy equine veterans are still patrolling streets in their 20s.

Though they work long hours, police horses receive top-notch care in precinct stables. Plus, they get lots of on-the-job perks—including friendly attention from citizens.

"My philosophy is that these horses work really hard and I like to keep them as sane as possible," Schramm says. "I think the horses tend to like people more if we let people reach out and touch them and feed them some grass or a carrot. It's a way to get to know the citizens and gain their trust. And citizens seem more inclined to approach a police officer on horseback. The horse gives them something to talk about—something to break the ice. Who in the world wants to pet a police car?"

Naturally, the long hours and inherent dangers of the job tend to strengthen the bond between horse and rider. "In most units, an officer and a horse are matched up and stay together for the duration of their assignment," says Schramm. "That way, they build confidence in one another and work as a team. They know what to expect from each other.

"After all, these animals are carrying our lives on their backs," she continues. "They're out there doing their job—a job that ensures everybody's safety. You can't ask much more than that from a horse."

from PETLIFE

Devil Dog

PFC PETER A. VOSS, USMC

---

*M*arines have been called devildogs since World War II, when Germans gave them the name in honor of their ferocious fighting ability. All marines share pride in this nickname, but one marine stationed at Camp Foster in Okinawa, Japan, gives the term new meaning.

Like his fellow soldiers, this marine has a military occupational specialty, a service record book, uniforms, a social security number, dog tags and medals. He has re-enlisted twice. But unlike most Marines, this devil dog has a special affinity for fire hydrants.

Donated in 1989, Chopper III immediately became the III Marine Expeditionary Force (III MEF) Band's mascot. The golden retriever enlisted in the Marine Corps as a private, when he was 20 pounds and 24 days old. In October 1998 he reached his current rank of staff sergeant, when General Charles C. Krulak, commandant of the Marine Corps, promoted him in a ceremony at Camp Foster.

This dog doesn't lie around the barracks. He has his own military occupational specialty—5569, duty howler. "He does his job very well," said Chief Warrant Officer James A. Ford, band officer of the III MEF Band. "He knows all the band members, and he'll growl at all the non-band members who come to the barracks." He also can do tricks that illustrate stealth, agility, discipline and intelligence: Chopper III can lie down and bark on command, decide what hand is holding a dog bone, and balance a dog bone on his nose, then catch it in his mouth on command.

Chopper III's Service Record Book (SRB) contains everything the typical Marine's does. An SRB is the record of a Marine's awards, administrative paperwork and other basic information. Through the years, Chopper III averaged a 4.7 rating, out of 5.0, in productivity and conduct marks. His predecessors have histories of urinating on the flagpole during flag-raising ceremonies and on officers' shoes, but Chopper III's page 11, where minor disciplinary infractions are recorded, consists only of one unauthorized absence—he disappeared overnight. All of the documents in the SRB are signed with Chopper III's paw print.

Chopper III has a Navy Unit Citation, Sea Service Deployment ribbon, Good Conduct Medal and the National Defense Medal. He has his own camouflage and dress blue uniforms, which are maintained by Lance Corporal Timothy A. Curling, the current mascot handler. Curling, a trumpet player with the band, also takes Chopper III out for physical training, washes him and feeds him.

"I volunteered for the job (of mascot handler) because I had a golden retriever at home, and Chopper III reminds me of him," said Curling. "It's just like having your own dog." Curling initially forgot how difficult it was taking care of an animal. "It's really hard, but it's all worth it," he noted. Part of Curling's responsibility includes taking Chopper III to the vet every three months. "The vet says we have been taking good care of him," said Curling.

That's good news because Chopper III was once over-weight and had to be put on a strict diet. "Band members used to feed him human food all the time," recalled Ford. "Now he only eats dog food, and only twice a day."

Chopper III knows when it's feeding time and when it's time to go to sleep, according to Corporal Matthew R. McKibbon, a trombone player in the band. "At 0700 (7 a.m.) and 1800 (6 p.m.), he will go to the duty noncommissioned officer (NCO) and nag him for his chow," said McKibbon. He does this by giving the duty NCO "the look." If the duty NCO ignores him, he performs a pouting routine until he gets fed. "Chopper III will go to the duty NCO when it's time to sleep, too," McKibbon said. Chopper's bed is in the same room where the duty NCO sleeps. Sometimes Chopper will follow the duty NCO around if he feels it is taking the duty NCO too long to go to bed.

Chopper III spends time with the band at almost every re-hearsal. Band members say they feel like he watches over them while they practice. "Sometimes he'll sing along with the band," said McKibbon. "I would say he has a good ear for music."

from DOG & KENNEL

How to Carry a Burden

MARY LOU CARNEY

$\mathcal{B}$efore our family acquired the old Farmall tractor, my father always plowed our garden with a team of horses. I remember the first time he harnessed Juniper to that one-bottom plow. Young and inexperienced, she twitched and pranced in the traces. Her partner Flighty stood quietly as Dad adjusted the final buckles. I sat on top of the garden gate and watched them make the rounds, the black ground breaking open with each pass. Juniper pulled and tugged; sweat soaked her coat. Flighty walked with a measured, methodical pace. By the end of the morning, Juniper was exhausted.

As Dad unhitched them, I commented on the difference in the two. Dad smiled. "Juniper's just new to this," he said. "When a young horse is first hooked to a team, he tries to pull the whole load. He wears himself out in no time. Soon Juniper'll learn to lay back and share the load."

Often I find myself, like that inexperienced horse, trying to pull the load alone. I fail to reach out for support. I pretend not to need the very assistance I am eager to offer others. By feigning self-sufficiency, I thwart God's ordained system of support and encouragement. So I've hung a reminder on my refrigerator door: *Burdens Are for Sharing.* I'm trying harder now not only to share the burdens of others, but also to let them share my burdens.

A Dog Named Silk

DONALD McCAIG

Whenever she leaves our farm, Silk doesn't know if she'll ever return. I am her fifth owner. More than once, this Border Collie has left her home and not come back to it.

Silk was an outright gift from her frustrated breeder, who knew that if Silk didn't work out as my trial dog, she'd still have a home for life with my family. Although her littermates were burning up the sheepdog trial circuit, at 3 years old Silk already had failed four times.

One of her prior owners—a good and gentle handler—gave up on Silk. "She was fine so long as she was working in the training field," she told me. "But the minute we were done, Silk'd take off back to the house, run right across the highway, wouldn't listen to me. I was afraid she'd be killed."

My wife, Anne, and I operated a 280-acre sheep farm in the Virginia mountains. We have five dogs, and night or day I never go to the sheep without a dog at my side. When lambs are born, we use a dog to bring them and their mothers into the barn. Dogs fetch sheep for feeding, worming, shearing and foot trimming. Our dogs sort sick sheep from the flock and bring them in for doctoring. When a neighbor's bull smashes through our wire fence en route to our heifer, the dogs dissuade him from his amour.

I've been training and trialing sheepdogs for almost 20 years and should be better at it than I am. At a 60-dog trial, I'm happy to place 10th—somewhere between the worst of the good runs and best of the mediocre ones. But 10th isn't good enough to qualify a dog for the National Finals. This year, however, my luck would change.

When Silk and I do everything perfectly we can persuade our sheep to go places sensible sheep would rather not. Sheep are a prey species and don't like to walk between gates or into a pen; to a sheep, gates and pens are traps. They fear approaching a strange human and the crowd of possibly dangerous spectator-humans standing behind them. They are spooked by wind or the sun in their eyes. Their flocking instinct is a deeply rooted survival strategy, and when a dog sorts a single ewe off from her pals, that single animal fears becoming an entree.

You cannot force sheep—they'll run over the dog or panic and bolt. (A young ewe can outsprint a dog for 100 yards or so.) What Silk and I hope to do together is quietly close off every other possibility so the sheep see the terrifying pen as the lesser evil and walk into it willingly.

Sheepdogs are as different from one another as people are. When she's not working, Silk's a goof: She flounces and rolls, picks up sticks and careens around with them. When she's working, however, she is intent and biddable, and she "reads" (understands) her sheep and paces them accordingly. She's got enough power to shift stubborn sheep and the courage to march into the face of a foot-stomping, head-lowered ewe protecting her newborn lamb.

When Silk came to my farm, she was stick-shy and wouldn't come near my shepherd's crook. She ran too wide—she'd head for the nearest fence and run along it until she got behind her sheep. She actually wasn't running to get sheep, she was relieving stress: running, running, running through a safe world of her own. We call her habit "running silly."

From 6 months of age Silk had been trained and retrained and trained again by her previous owners, and the first time I sent her to gather a flock of 100 ewes—a task any farm sheep-dog can accomplish—Silk got to the sheep and they drifted while she waited for my command. She never had been al-lowed to think for herself and didn't know how.

Silk was terrified of riding in the car, and windshield wipers drove her onto the floorboards, trembling. She was overweight and so indifferent to self-grooming, Anne named her "Dirty Girty." After haymaking on hot summer afternoons, I'd take all our dogs down to the river for a swim. Silk wouldn't go in the water.

Farm work relaxes sheepdogs and increases their confi-dence, so Silk became our "chore dog." I used her for routine tasks—fetching the ewes in for feed, driving them back to pas-ture—low-stress work without many commands. I'd send her on "blind" outruns—into pasture where the grass was so tall neither of us could see the sheep. Silk had to find them; she had to bring them back. She had to start thinking for herself. Whenever we worked together, I carried my crook hoping she'd lose her fear of it.

I didn't do much formal training. She already had been trained to her limits. Slowly and patiently I showed Silk she could trust me and that she was my dog. Six months after we got her, Silk was swimming with the other dogs, and about half the time she'd make a decent outrun. Without any change in diet, she'd become trim, and nowadays she kept herself well-groomed.

It took time, but eventually Silk trusted me enough that I could use my stick at a trial. On the crossdrive at a Pennsylvania trial, trial-savvy sheep suckered dog after dog out of position as they neared the crossdrive gates, and when the dog couldn't catch them, the sheep bolted off the course. The dogs subsequently were disqualified with scores of zero. But Silk paced her sheep so quietly that they were lulled, and when they finally bolted it was too late—Silk caught them and put them through the gates.

Ours had been a pretty run, but a slow one. From the sidelines Miss Ethel cried, "Hurry up, Donald!" When we reached the pen, the sheep balked, and one thought to run over me so I dropped to my knees—eye to eye with the animal—and explained who was the predator species and who was the prey. With two seconds to spare, the sheep went in the pen, and Silk won her first blue ribbon. We were qualified for the National Handler's Finals.

At our qualifying run, Silk left my feet running silly. The brush didn't keep her on the course, she ran through it like a gasping, over-stressed hurdler, and when she came behind her sheep she was disoriented. Her sheep missed the fetch gates and when they came around the post Silk went out too wide and had no control at all. So I tipped my hat to the judge, and Silk and I retired.

I felt terrible. Later that evening, a fellow who'd come as far as I had and also was disqualified said, "Look at it this way. If you add up all the hurt and disappointment and divide by the miles traveled, on a per-mile basis, it doesn't amount to much."

Thanks so very much.

Three days later, I was driving across the last mountain before my farm. Since Silk came to me a year and a half ago she'd made a lot of progress. Silk was my dog now.

Well, I guess we had more work to do. We'd just have to fix her outrun.

When I turned at the top of our farm lane, Silk—who never barked—started barking in joy and pleasure, "Bark, bark, bark, bark." Silk, the dog who'd had so many homes, finally was coming home.

from DOG WORLD

The Language of Horses

MONTY ROBERTS, as told to CAROL KLINE

$\mathcal{M}$y father, a traditional horseman, was a tough authoritarian. He used intimidation and brutality to "break" horses to his will. Unfortunately, he used the same methods on me. At eight years old, after witnessing a particularly vicious example of my father's methods, I vowed that my life would be different. I would use communication, not violence, to enlist the cooperation of the horses I trained. I was sure that horses had a language, and if I could speak that language, I could train horses in a new and entirely different way. So it was at the age of eight that I set a life goal for myself—to be able to communicate fluently with horses.

My father thought this idea was nonsense, so I had to pursue my goal without his help. My mother supported me, but secretly, for she also feared my father's anger. We lived on a horse facility in Salinas, California, at the time, and I spent every waking hour trying to communicate with the untamed domestic horses on the facility.

The summer I was thirteen, I went to Nevada for three weeks for a job. I had been hired to capture wild mustangs. This was the first opportunity I'd had to work with totally wild horses. Determined to make the best use of my time, I rose early each day and rode a long way into the desert, where I used binoculars to study the habits of the mustang herds that lived there.

I was utterly spellbound by these horses. I would sit for hours and hours, watching those beautiful animals as they ran, grazed and played in the wide spaces of the desert.

What astonished me most was how the wild horses communicated with each other. They rarely used sounds; instead, they used a complex language of motion. The position of their bodies, and the speed and direction of their travel were the key elements of their language. And by varying the degree of rigidity or relaxation in the eyes, ears, neck, head and position of the spine, a horse could signal anything it needed to communicate.

As I watched, I thought: *Could I convince a wild horse to let me get close enough to touch him without him running away?*

For easy spotting, I picked a horse with unique markings, and tried to herd him away from the others. For many days I tried every way I could think of to get near him, but he always sensed me and he was off before I was even close. One day, I got lucky and came up behind him in a small canyon. At last, I had his full attention. Then, using only my body to convey the signals I'd seen the horses use with each other, I persuaded the wary stallion to stand still. He watched me silently as I moved closer and closer. He was watchful, but he wasn't afraid. Not breathing, I took the step that brought me within an arm's reach of him. I avoided his eyes as I stretched my hand toward him and laid it softly on his neck. It lasted only a few seconds, but it was enough. I watched him gallop away, my chest exploding with joy. I had communicated with a horse!

When I returned home, I was bursting with excitement

and told my mother what had happened in the desert with the mustang. While I could see that she was happy for me, all she said was that I must never speak of it to my father or anyone else, or I would get in trouble. I felt let down, but I knew she was right. My desire to learn to communicate with horses became a deep inner passion that I fiercely hid from the rest of the world.

Unable to share what was most important to me with anyone, I was almost always alone, except for the horses. The only thing that mattered to me was my life's dream.

Every summer, I returned to Nevada for three weeks to work, continuing my research in the desert. Four years later, when I was seventeen, I progressed so far that I not only touched a wild mustang, I saddled, bridled and rode one without once using any pain or intimidation to do so. Proudly, I rode the wild horse back to the ranch. The ranch hands who saw me ride in called me a liar when I told them what I'd done. They ridiculed me and insisted the horse I rode must once have been a domesticated horse who had run away and ended up with the mustangs. Deeply hurt, I realized the futility of my dreams. With no one to believe in me, it was *my* spirit that was broken.

I eventually got over the pain of that devastating humiliation and decided to continue my training methods, but I vowed I would never again tell anyone what I did.

And so I became a horse trainer. I used my experience with every horse I worked with to learn more and more about the language of horses. It was a slow but satisfying education.

Once, when I was about twenty-five, a family hired me to tackle the problem of their mare, My Blue Heaven. She was a beautiful horse, intelligent and extremely talented. But during her training, a previous owner had inadvertently mishandled her and she had developed a serious problem: She wouldn't stop. She would blast away like a rocket and refuse to be halted—crashing through fences, and slipping and sliding as she made dangerously sharp turns. She was diabolically treacherous. A short time earlier, the mare had almost killed the present owner's daughter. The family was going on vacation and they asked me to sell the horse for them for whatever I could get for her. They had heard I was good with difficult horses and they knew in order to sell her, someone would have to be able to bring her to a stop from a run. No one else was willing to try.

She was the most dangerous horse I had ever seen, but I used everything I had absorbed over the years to help her. Moving slowly and keeping my communication with her to just the basics, I earned her trust. Building on that trust, I continued to communicate with her, and soon she melted. Our progress was swift and remarkable from that point on. It had seemed impossible, but within a few days, she was transformed.

While the owners were still away, I showed her in a competition and she took first place. I brought her prize, a very expensive saddle, to the home of the family who still owned her. I wrote them a note, explaining that she had improved enough to win this saddle and under the circumstances, I felt that they should reconsider selling her. I pinned the note to the saddle and left it in the dining room for them to find upon their return.

They were ecstatic about the change in My Blue Heaven and were thrilled to be able to keep her. My Blue Heaven went on to become a world-class champion. And her owners found in her a new willingness and sweet temper that made her presence in their family even more precious than her show value.

My Blue Heaven was one of my first public triumphs. But

this same story repeated itself over and over during the next thirty years. Hopeless cases were referred to me, and using the simple tools of gentleness, respect and communication, I managed to turn them around.

By then, it was hard to keep my work secret. Even though I still met with some skepticism and scorn, I found many more who were open to, and enthusiastic about, what I was doing.

I was particularly well received in England. In fact, in 1989, I was astounded to find myself, the son of an American horse trainer, being presented to Her Royal Majesty, Elizabeth II, queen of England. It had been a long and often painful road from the high deserts of Nevada to the splendor of Windsor Castle.

That was the turning point of my career. The queen then endorsed my methods and provided me with her private car to tour England and demonstrate my techniques all over the country. Today, it is even possible to study my methods of horse training at West Oxfordshire College in England.

I have achieved what I set out to do when I was a boy of eight. But I feel that I am just a scout, marking the trail for all who will follow me. I watch the young people who are studying my work, and I know they will carry it forward to achieve communication with horses I can't even begin to imagine.

In a certain way, I have my father to thank for setting my life on this course. Out of his work with horses, my passion for them began. And from his violence, my dream was born— that all horses be spared the needless pain and suffering of being "broken."

from CHICKEN SOUP FOR THE PET LOVER'S SOUL

Bo's World

JOE KIRKUP

$\mathcal{M}$ost of my memories of Vietnam are the kind that jerk my breath away at 3 a.m. and leave me clenching my fists, waiting for the blessed light of dawn. We all made choices we now must live with. How many bullets versus how much water? When the rescue chopper says "only three" and there are four of you, do you leave a guy or "lock and load" on the pilot? Worst of all, when it's dark and nobody can help, do you let some mangled kid die slowly or just get it over with? In all the darkness of that time, however, there was one bright spot: a big German shepherd named Bo.

Bo was a scout dog for my infantry unit. His mission was to sniff out Viet Cong guerrillas, their tunnels, ammo caches and booby traps. Like the rest of us, he was a soldier on the outside and a puppy in his heart.

Occasionally, our unit would stop for a few days to guard some smoldering mechanized unit or back up a Special Forces team. While we waited, Bo would entertain us with his skills. His handler would tie a thin monofilament across a path, then dare guys to step over it. Bo's job was to stop us. He'd been taught it was better to eat one GI than let him trigger a mine that popped into the air and detonated at the level of everybody's head.

I would pet Bo and let him begin eating my C-rations. Then I'd start toward the string. Bo was never won over by my ham steak. As I approached the tripwire, he'd race ahead, then turn toward me, flattening his radar-station ears and rolling gravy-moistened lips. Bone-crushing teeth would appear. His huge torso would sink into a crouch as he prepared to spring. In 'Nam we dealt with pretty scary stuff, but when Bo told you to stop, no one had the guts to take a step.

The minute I backed off, Bo and I would be pals again. "Sit, Bo. You want a goody?" Sure he did. In those big brown eyes you could read his thoughts: *I'm glad I didn't have to kill this jerk before I got the rest of his C-rats.*

One steamy, miserable day my unit was moving through light jungle and tall trees. I was fourth from point. Bo and his handler were behind me.

Gunshots, their sharpness blunted by the smothering humidity, exploded around us. We hit the vine-covered jungle floor. "In the trees! In the trees!" someone hissed.

More shots came, louder now. Beside me, Bo flinched. I emptied three 20-round clips in the direction of the noise. My frantic and scruffy peers did likewise. When the smoke cleared, a body was hanging out of a tree.

Bo seemed all right. We made him roll over and stand up. Then I saw that line of slick, dark blue-red we all knew too well.

A bullet had pierced Bo's foreleg. It appeared to be a clean hole, bleeding only slightly. When I patted him, he wagged his tail. His sad, intelligent eyes seemed to be saying, "It's okay, Joe. I'm not important. I'm just here to protect you."

A chopper took Bo away. As I smoothed his fur good-bye, I wondered if they would send the big guy home. But in a few weeks, to my joy and sorrow, he was back.

Midsummer. We were 1000 meters from a huge field outside a tiny hamlet, Sui Tres. In the field was an artillery unit. Around them were 2500 VC. Our job was to shoot our way through and secure the howitzer guys.

The night before, we slept on the jungle floor, lying with our heads on our helmets and trying not to notice what crawled over us. Just before dawn, the unsteady rumble of machine-gun and heavy-weapons fire erupted from the direction of Sui Tres. Time to face the devil.

I put on my helmet and grabbed my gear. Bo wandered over to see if we had time for breakfast. Around me the dark jungle was filled with muttered curses and rustling equipment.

Suddenly Russian-made rockets streaked through the treetops overhead. I heard what sounded like escaping steam, followed by a long moment of silence. Then deafening, lung-crushing thunder.

Dust filled the air. I was face-down on the ground, not knowing how I got there. People were screaming for medics. My helmet, split open by shrapnel, no longer fit on my head.

Through the confusion, I saw Bo's long black tail wagging. He was crouched beside his handler, waiting for orders. But the young soldier's right shoulder and most of his chest were gone. White dust covered his corpse and the dog beside him.

I pulled Bo gently toward me and stroked the fur on his back. Sticky liquid covered my hand and ran down the side of his body. A tiny piece of shrapnel had penetrated his back below the spine. He seemed not to notice, and again pulled toward his handler. "He didn't make it," I told Bo, holding the dog against my chest. "He just didn't make it."

Each GI was issued a large cloth bandage. The rule was to use your buddy's bandage for him and save yours for yourself.

Bo didn't have a bandage, so I wrapped him in mine.

We put the dead and wounded—humans and canine—on choppers and went on to kill 641 VC before the day was over. I never saw Bo again.

September 18, 1967. I was processing out of 'Nam. Malaria had reduced me from 165 to 130 pounds. I looked and felt like a corpse in combat boots. My heart was filled with death: the smell, the look, the wrenching finality of it. After 11 months and 29 days, it was time to go.

Standing in line, I began talking to the guy in front of me. He'd been a dog handler, he said. Now he was going home to his family's farm in Iowa. "It's a beautiful place," he said. "I never thought I'd live to see it again."

I told him about the scout dog I'd befriended—describing the huge, courageous shepherd and how he'd been shot. The soldier's next words took my breath away.

"You mean Bo!" he exclaimed.

"Yeah, how'd you know?"

"They gave him to me after my dog got killed."

For a moment I was happy. Then two miserable thoughts popped into my brain. First, I'd have to ask what had happened to Bo. Second, this handler was on his way home, leaving that loyal mutt to stay here until his luck ran out.

"So," I said hesitantly, staring at the toe of my boot, "what happened to that dog?"

The soldier lowered his voice the way people do when they have bad news. "He's gone."

I was so sick of death I thought I would throw up. Nothing seemed worth the life of that beautiful animal. I just wanted to sit down on the floor and cry. I guess the guy noticed my clenched fists and the wetness in my eyes. After looking around nervously, he lowered his voice again.

"Not dead, man," he said. "*Gone.* I got my company commander to fill out a death certificate, and we sent Bo back to my parents. He's been there for two weeks. Bo is back in Iowa."

What that skinny farm kid and his commanding officer did may not mean much to all those anti-war college kids who now control the newspapers and TV. And it may not have had the impact of the choices made by the now-remorseful Robert McNamara.

But it represents what was really in all our hearts. Of all the decisions made in Vietnam, this is the one I can live with.

from READER'S DIGEST

SPECIAL CARE

*"There is a bond between humans
and animals that is as undeniable and
immeasurable as the amount of
love a heart can hold."*

JACK HANNA

There was a time when an illness or a disability meant that people had to limit their way of life. Sometimes, because they couldn't do what most of us take for granted—walking, using stairs, picking things up, hearing a doorbell or a telephone, simply seeing what went on around them—they had to give up their independence and seek custodial care long before they needed it.

But not now. Today a disability can mean that, with the help of a specially trained animal, people can still have full lives—and all the love they can handle.

Murfee

SHERRY BENNETT WARSHAUER

---

*M*urfee is the first dog in the country certified by the American Red Cross to comfort disaster victims. Working in partnership with owner and nurse/therapist Carolyn Uhlin, he comforts hospital and mental clinic patients recovering from illness and injury, participates in after-school programs to help children with mental disabilities and is a regular visitor at nursing homes. . . .

Murfee is a very large, 105-pound, male yellow Lab. He was trained for his new career by Carolyn. Murfee is the third big yellow Lab Carolyn has used as a therapy dog. Keeping a uniform appearance among the dogs helps provide consistency for long-term patients. She wanted a dog that patients could reach from their hospital beds, enabling them to pet him.

Carolyn works for the Guilford County Medical Center, where she cares for people who suffer with depression, bi-polar disorder, anxiety disorders and schizophrenia. Murfee steps into situations where people feel as if they are losing control. His presence and his low-key personality are stabilizers that calm them in a matter of minutes. They go from being out of control to being able to speak, function and express themselves appropriately. Patients see the trust that Carolyn and Murfee have in each other. Once they come to trust Murfee, their trust is then transferred to Carolyn. Murfee represents unconditional love.

Murfee has interrupted patients experiencing a panic attack and has helped them calm down enough to get past it. Patients focus on the dog and relax. Even the most psychotic patients have maintained some lucidity with Murfee present.

He has had a profound effect on patient and family alike. When all else is forgotten, they remember Murfee. He adds a sense of normalcy to this sequence in their life. He also reduces the daily stress level of the staff.

A young child under the age of 10 was brought into the mental health department of an outpatient facility, fully restrained. The child was unable to speak, scared to death and out of control. As Carolyn walked by the child, she said, "Would you like to see my dog?" The child immediately perked up. In less than five minutes, Carolyn had the child out of restraints, talking to her and holding her hand and Murfee's leash. Sometime later, when it came time for this child to see the physician, Carolyn had to go and wake him up, for he had fallen asleep, cuddled up with Murfee on the floor. The child had his head on Murfee's belly, and both were quietly snoring. Murfee's ability to calm a person that quickly is remarkable.

An elderly patient was recovering from a stroke. She was bedridden and kept trying to reach for things. Carolyn would go in and visit regularly. One day, Carolyn entered her room and introduced Murfee to her. After a few tries, the woman repeated Murfee's name. Carolyn stuck her head out the door and asked the staff to come to the door and listen. The patient not only repeated the dog's name but told Carolyn how beautiful he was, as the eyes of the staff filled with tears. This patient had not spoken a word in five years.

from EVERYDAY HEROES

Jocko—at Your Service

MARILYN MESI PONA

I'll never forget what it was like to be disabled. And to need a helpful companion at my side.

Some time back I suffered through six years of intense back pain. Scoliosis had deformed my right hip and put me first on crutches, then in a wheelchair. I'd always been an active person, and losing my mobility was frustrating. I was constantly dropping socks and pens and utensils that were impossible for me to pick up. My life was strewn with objects I couldn't reach, doors I couldn't maneuver through, tiny chores I couldn't manage. My husband and three children helped me as much as possible, but they couldn't be with me all the time.

At last, doctors operated and removed pieces of ruptured disks that had twisted a nerve in my spine. The excruciating pain was gone. I could walk again! I went home, thanking God for my recovery.

But the energy I had mustered to fight the pain swirled inside me with no place to go. My children were growing up and busy with activities of their own; my husband had his job. Now what would fill *my* time?

I tried gardening, joined clubs, volunteered at animal shelters, took walks with my Labrador retriever, Max. But nothing challenged me. I couldn't help feeling there was some project that I was meant to do. I'd prayed for help during my time of pain, and I prayed now for guidance.

And then a news item about Sandy Maze of Columbus, Ohio, appeared on television. Sandy, who had muscular dystrophy, had paid a trainer to teach her dog, Stormy, to help her with simple but important tasks, such as retrieving keys, pencils and other objects. With Stormy's help, Sandy had been able to get around on her own, to lead a fuller, richer life, and even attend college. The experiment had worked so well that Sandy had started a group called Support Dogs for the Handicapped so that others could benefit from having a dog like hers.

I was thrilled! Here were the "friends" that could give an invaluable helping hand—or paw—to handicapped or disabled people. And here was the challenge I had been looking for. I picked up the phone and called Sandy. I'd start a group of my own in St. Louis!

With Sandy's long-distance encouragement and advice, I actually was able to train Max to pick up objects, to prop open doors, to carry the phone receiver to and from its cradle, and to help me get in and out of my wheelchair.

Soon I was speaking to local groups and organizations, explaining how useful support dogs could be. If I could arouse interest and raise money for a nonprofit organization in the St. Louis area, then I could educate others and help train dogs for handicapped people who might not otherwise know about or be able to afford training a dog on their own.

People listened sympathetically—but found it hard to understand how such a program would work in a *practical* way. My words weren't enough. I needed a dog right up there with me to demonstrate.

I tried to use Max. But Max didn't like the crowds and would freeze or retreat into the wings.

I *had* to have another dog. I talked to breeders, went to dog shows, answered ads in the paper. I saw sleek dogs, fuzzy dogs, well-bred dogs, frisky dogs—all handsome and well-groomed. But they were too high-strung, or too skittery, or too lackadaisical. No, not one animal I "interviewed" seemed right. But somehow I sensed that God had a dog waiting for me out there—a special dog.

And then one day while I was visiting the Open Door Animal Sanctuary in House Springs, about twenty miles from my home, I passed the pen where puppies were kept.

And there sitting stoically among the bouncing, rollicking pups, was a huge mound of a grown-up dog, with large, dark eyes and a penetrating gaze.

At first I almost laughed out loud. On my second look, I almost wept. I can't remember seeing a more road-worn, tattered animal. The dog was scarred and bruised, but his big brown eyes seemed to be telling me something.

"What are you doing here with the puppies?" I asked. His tail gave a thump. As I walked away, I knew he was watching me.

"That's Jocko," the girl in the office told me. "Or at least that's what we're calling him." He'd been found wandering on the highway. He was part Great Dane, part retriever, around four years old and probably had been abused. "We had to put him in with the puppies," the girl explained, "because he kept jumping our fences, and the puppies' pen is the only one that's covered."

I walked back to the pen. On closer inspection, poor Jocko looked not better, but *worse*. An infection had eaten away part of one ear. And when, with an apologetic air, he leaned back to scratch, I saw that his paw pads were raw.

He was a mess. Who would ever think of adopting such a dog?

God would. *Look beyond the outward appearance,* a voice inside me whispered. *This dog is special. This is the one you've been looking for.*

I took Jocko for a "test run," walking along the road. He wasn't spooked by roaring cars or sudden noises or new people, and he seemed alert and easygoing.

When I took him home, the rest of the family was aghast.

"*That's* the new dog?"

"Gosh, he's a mess."

"Support dog? He doesn't look like he could support himself."

And then my husband drove up, took one look out the car window, and drove off in mock horror. After circling the block, he returned, and got out to gape. "You've got to be kidding," he said.

But Jocko didn't seem at all concerned that he wasn't getting the "Beautiful Pet of the Year" award. He wagged his tail, and by the next day all I heard was, "We're keeping that nice dog, aren't we?"

I scrubbed him up, gave him his medicine, and just two days later took him to a muscular dystrophy camp. Jocko quickly became the center of attention, and loved it. He didn't cringe or snap when eager-but-uncoordinated hands reached out to pet or hug him. And if it was awkward for a person in a wheelchair to reach him, he would maneuver his head under that hand. Ah, this was the temperament I had been searching for.

Now how would he take to training? Well, he didn't have

to be taught to be a ham. On Halloween he went trick-or-treating, carrying a purse in his mouth and acting as if he had done it all his life.

But what about the specifics and disciplines of training? I started by teaching him simple commands like "come," "stay," "heel," "sit" and "stand," using both voice and hand signals. I helped things along by hooking Jocko's leash to Max's collar; when Max performed his own retrieval tasks, Jocko was pulled right along.

The weeks went by. Jocko had to be trained not just to pick up an object, but also to hold on until a hand was ready to take it. Picking up a telephone receiver was one thing—but if the receiver was dropped halfway across the room, it didn't do a handicapped person much good. Over and over and over again I worked with Jocko, sometimes assisted by Max, until Jocko got the point: Pick up an object and carry it to the waiting person's hand.

Nine months passed. Jocko's appearance underwent a startling transformation. His emaciated frame filled out, his coat started to shine. His once-infected cauliflower ear was still scrunched in, but now he stood tall and had a spring in his step.

Jocko was ready for his first demonstration. I took him before a group of rambunctious second-graders. As Jocko retrieved a pencil, an eraser and assorted other objects, the youngsters watched in rapt attention. And they burst into applause when Jocko helped me out of a chair by pulling me up as I hung on to his leash. Jocko's performance was flawless; I said a silent prayer of thanks. This *was* the special dog God had intended for me.

Soon Jocko and I were doing two to four demonstrations a week. He would pick up my cane, my keys—even a dime. He would help me up steps, or stand still and firm so that I could show how someone who had fallen could use a dog as a brace to get up.

By now people were asking for "the lady with the big yellow dog." Jocko had become a pro, ready and willing to be petted, talked to and photographed.

Over the following months, more and more people were able to *see* how helpful—even essential—a dog could be to a handicapped person.

Bit by bit, people offered money, time, skills and services. In May 1983, Support Dogs for the Handicapped was officially incorporated in St. Louis as a nonprofit organization. And Jocko's stardom continued to grow when he was nominated as Service Dog of the Year. But in spite of his newfound fame, he still kept all four feet on the ground: Whenever I had a relapse and my back acted up again, Jocko still acted as my support dog. He literally gave me a boost and eased my way.

Again and again Jocko rose to the occasion. And because of him, a whole new battalion of dogs and a lot of puppies are doing the same. Today, in addition to the adult dogs that our group trains, we also breed the most suitable dogs and will start training puppies at the earliest possible age.

I think back to eight years ago. A raggedy old pooch and a frustrated former invalid—both of us needing something to do. And I thank God, who got us together and turned us into a golden dog and an active lady, eager to let you know that, no matter how bent over or beat up you are, you too can rise to the occasion. And have the full, rich life God intends you to have.

You can bet a pen full of puppies on it.

Meet Flopsy

DONNA BOETIG

It was Ginny Cornett's first day at the Shriner's Burn Institute in Galveston, Tex., working as a therapist using animals to help burned children. Beside her was her partner, a rabbit named Flopsy. The pair had been sent by Moody Gardens, an educational and entertainment complex that takes animals to hospitals and nursing homes.

Their first patient was a three-year-old girl suffering from third-degree burns. She was wrapped from head to toe in bandages; two holes were cut for her nose and mouth. Her eyes were blinded by gauze.

"I have a friend I want you to meet," Cornett said. "This is Flopsy." She lightly brushed the rabbit against the only exposed part of the girl's body, the bottom of one foot. After a few strokes, the child sank her toes into the rabbit's soft fur, squealing with glee.

Flopsy is a favorite with the kids at Shriner's, who find release from their pain in weekly sessions with the rabbit. They also gain comfort from the animal's unusual appearance. Flopsy is a New Zealand white rabbit with pink eyes and one floppy ear. Her unspoken message—that looking different isn't bad—helps her patients accept their disfigurements.

Last year Flopsy and Cornett flew to New York to receive the 1997 Delta Society National Award for Animal-Assisted Therapy. Sharing the spotlight with stars like fashion designer Carolina Herrera made little impression on the rabbit. Instead, she longingly eyed the floral centerpieces, which brimmed with fresh greenery.

from McCALL'S

A Perfect Roommate

ED AND TONI EAMES

Prologue to Act 1, Scene 1. Curtain rises on a hospital room. Center stage is a bed in which a middle-aged woman is lying down. Door at back of room opens and cleaning woman enters. She greets patient, places her cleaning equipment near the bed and, as she moves in front of the bed, her face shows amazement as a large Golden Retriever stands up and greets her with tail wagging. The look of amazement gives way to a look of delight as she moves forward to pet the dog.

If this reads like the prologue to a play destined to open on Broadway, think again. This is not fiction; it is a real-life drama and portrays the scene in my hospital room on Thursday, March 26, 1998. The actual setting is St. Agnes Medical Center in Fresno, Calif. I am the middle-aged patient in bed. Escort, my guide dog, is the wagging Golden Retriever who greeted this hospital employee.

In mid-February, I discovered a small lump in my left breast, and subsequent tests indicated it was suspicious. In early March, a surgical biopsy confirmed the radiologist's suspicion that the lump was malignant. Because my mother and two maternal aunts had breast cancer, I was not unprepared for this diagnosis. I was in a high-risk category, and the risk had become a reality.

My surgeon, Dr. Meg Hadcock, suggested the preferred treatment was mastectomy. Realizing the surgery could not be delayed for long, I negotiated with Dr. Hadcock for a two-week postponement during which my husband, Ed, and I could meet our lecturing commitments. We were scheduled to take a 12-day trip to do presentations at Tuskegee University, Auburn University and the University of Missouri veterinary schools, a national veterinary student conference at the University of Florida and the veterinary technician program at St. Petersburg Community College.

During this trip, I stayed in close contact with Dr. Hadcock, who responded sympathetically to my fears and concerns. I was one of those rare but fortunate Americans whose hospital experiences previously had been limited to visiting others. My only prior hospitalization was 51 years ago, when, at age 3, my tonsils were removed. Dr. Hadcock empathized with my need to not be separated from Escort during this traumatic time. She assured me that arrangements would be made to permit him to stay with me at St. Agnes.

Based on prior discussions with Joe Langan, St. Agnes Medical Center's executive vice president, I knew this facility had a progressive assistance dog policy. On previous occasions when Ed and I, accompanied by our guide dogs, visited hospitalized friends, Mr. Langan, an Irish Setter fancier, always welcomed us. Like Dr. Hadcock, he recognized the therapeutic and healing value of having Escort with me during my hospital stay.

Before entering the hospital, several dog-related plans had to be made. I packed dog food and bowls for both Escort and Echo, Ed's guide dog. Wanting Escort to recognize this as a work rather than a play setting, I did not bring toys. For those times Ed would be with me, relief breaks would be no problem. Friends Beth Shea and Linda Haymond were to take on this chore while spending the night with me. Ed had to return home to care for Kismet, Nifty and Bonzie, the feline members of the family.

On the day of surgery, my friend Helen Shea picked Ed and me up at the crack of dawn to drive us to St. Agnes. When we arrived, Escort assumed his position at my left side and proudly guided me inside. Intake staff greeted him like an old friend. Three weeks earlier, he had become a noteworthy visitor while accompanying me during pre-op appointments. I glowed as receptionists, technicians and nurses greeted him by name.

After being checked in and receiving my identification bracelet, Helen, Ed and I were ushered into the waiting room. Not knowing how long it would take to be a functioning team again, I gave Escort lots of hugs and whispered reassuring words into his soft, floppy ears. Of course, this physical contact also served to reassure me. Before long, the pre-op nurse came to fetch me, and I left Escort with Ed in the waiting room.

Following completion of the necessary paperwork, I was hooked up to an IV line, blood pressure machine and other monitoring devices. Ed, Helen and the Golden boys then were summoned to join me. Escort approached my bed, and I was able to cuddle him until the surgical team appeared. Dr. Hadcock greeted Escort and assured him our separation would be brief. As they wheeled me into the surgical suite, I felt reassured knowing Ed and Escort would be there when I woke up.

During the two-hour surgical procedure, Ed and Helen settled down in the waiting room. They shared feelings of anxiety and stress with others waiting for loved ones to emerge from surgery. Many of those fellow waiters sought permission to cuddle the Goldens. Invariably, a slight lessening of the tension could be felt as these well-wishers interacted with the boys. A young brother and sister waiting for their grandpa's return derived particular delight in the presence of these available canine stress relievers. Their mom also was pleased to have their youthful energy diverted in such a constructive fashion.

As I came out of my anesthesia-induced fog, my first sensations were of Ed patting my hand and Escort butting me with his nose. As prearranged by Dr. Hadcock, I was in a private room. Although barely awake, I directed Ed where to place Escort's Mutt Mat. Last year when Escort and I earned highest-scoring local Novice Dog in the Fresno Training Club's American Kennel Club-sanctioned obedience trial, this mat was our trophy. Unused until now, it became home base for Escort. Initially, he wanted to sleep next to my bed, but we were concerned he would become tangled in the IV line and would be in the way of nurses needing to get to my bedside. Ed showed Escort the mat and requested him to do a Down/Stay on it. Amazingly, after this initiation, he needed no coaxing to return to his assigned resting place. Always wanting to be in control, I was pleased with how smoothly things were progressing.

Keeping St. Agnes' open-door assistance dog policy in mind, I wanted Escort to demonstrate exemplary manners and decorum in the hospital. At home, he greets friends with extreme exuberance, emitting high-pitched squeals of delight. I also permit him to bark when someone comes to the door. Because many of his favorite people would be visiting, I was concerned he might exhibit too much enthusiasm when greeting these guests. I hoped he would not bark when hospital personnel knocked on the door or entered the room. Not to worry! Sensing the need to be on his best behavior, Escort was the picture of the true professional. Although not in harness, he greeted everyone calmly and quietly with a controlled, wagging tail.

One of those visitors, and one of Escort's special friends, was Marsha Eichholtz, who, along with her husband, Doug Low, operate what has become Fresno's most renowned cookie shop. On each day of my stay, Marsha supplied three dozen of her delicious cookies. She believed that between the allure of her Doug-Out Cookies and the presence of two Golden Retrievers, the nursing staff would be drawn like magnets to my room! She was right!

After Ed and Echo left for the day, Beth settled in for the night. She fed Escort and took him out for his final relief break. Because visitors and nurses had not consumed all the Doug-Out Cookies, Beth was able to bring a supply to the night security guards. When Beth and Escort did not return to the room within what I considered a reasonable period, I began to worry. On her return, Beth reminded me that time had to be set aside for the security staff to have a therapeutic cuddle session with my lovable canine partner. On the second night when Linda took on night duty, I was prepared for their long absence when Escort was taken out for his final relief break.

During the day when people were in and out of my room, Escort would get up and greet them. When nurse Mary Ellen tiptoed in at 5 a.m. to take my vital signs, however, Escort thought this still was the middle of the night and simply wagged his tail while remaining stretched out on the mat.

from DOG WORLD

Seeing-Eye Person

ARTHUR GORDON

A letter came today from our friend George who lives in the shadow of the Whitestone Bridge on the edge of New York City. In one paragraph he talks about his friend Co-co.

Co-co is a big chocolate-colored poodle, the most remarkable dog I've ever met. Whenever we'd come to visit, Co-co would astonish us by seeming to understand every word George said to her. If he wanted his shoes from upstairs, she'd go and get them. If they were the wrong pair, she'd take them back and bring the right one. If George said, "Robber!" or "Crook!" she'd go tearing around the house to make sure there were no intruders. Now and then I'd see Co-co and George looking at each other with affectionate amusement, as if they shared a joke that none of the rest of us could understand.

But the years go by, and now George's letter says—and I know it was painful for him to write—that Co-co has gone blind. "We've evolved a way of looping her leash (which she hasn't worn in years) loosely around her shoulders, and with this she walks confidently by my side. I can steer her either way with the slightest pressure. So here I am, a seeing-eye person for a blind dog."

Now on afternoons like today with so many angry headlines in the paper and so many small problems crowding in,

I somehow find it both touching and heartening to think of my friend George and his friend Co-co walking along tranquilly and trustfully, side by side. And I know the leash is only a symbol of the real bond between them.

The real bond is love.

The Big
Teddy Bear

SALLY DENEEN

$\mathcal{B}$ella the Golden Retriever always seemed to know when Carol Roquemore was upset. Bella nuzzled her bent knee to provoke a smile or dropped a toy on her lap as if to say: "Wanna play?"

Having contracted polio at age 4, a grown-up Roquemore of Perris, Calif., relied on Bella, her service dog, to hand clerks credit cards and cash. Bella picked out coins as specific as a dime or quarter, flipped light switches and retrieved the phone. One stunning call asked Roquemore to reach into her heart and make a difficult decision—to send Bella to live with someone who needed her dog's help even more.

Heather Adams had an inoperable brain tumor. She lost use of her legs, hands and arms. The sudden tumor sent her family reeling. Would she continue to be able to live independently? Living on her own was a matter of pride for Adams, born with cerebral palsy but managing life on her own today in Nipomo, Calif., at age 24.

Doctors once told Adams she had a year to live. Due to her cerebral palsy, she was on a two-year waiting list for a service dog from Canine Support Teams Inc., a Perris-based, non-profit organization for which Roquemore is CEO and Training Supervisor. But the life-threatening tumor made getting a canine helper urgent.

"She could hardly crawl, it was so bad," recalled Adams' mother, Jacque Murray, who was determined to find a solution. "It was like, 'Omigosh, what are we going to do?'"

Roquemore picked up the phone and heard Murray ask: "Is there any way at all, can she have a dog now?"

It was particularly unfortunate timing. Service dogs need six to eight months of training to meet the needs of a specific disabled person. During this time, the dogs go through repeated evaluations including health, temperament and performance. The latest string of four-legged trainees had already graduated from Roquemore's program—leaving none for Adams.

"It broke my heart," Roquemore said. "It was a very sad thing." She hung up the phone. "After I had a good cry, I called her mother back and said, 'I think we have a dog for Heather.'" Adams wept tears of joy upon seeing her surprise gift—Bella—on her birthday, Jan. 31.

"She was absolutely overwhelmed," Murray said. "She never thought she'd get a dog. It was a gift of the heart. Bella is even more special because of that." At first, Murray resisted taking Roquemore's service dog; but Roquemore insisted.

Since then, three years have passed. Adams, exuding enthusiasm as she beamed about her latest computer classes, said she looked forward to getting a part-time job working with computers or animals.

As soon as Bella showed up at her home, Adams felt happier. "I was going through radiation—I was really tired, and I didn't want to get up or do anything," Adams said. But with

Bella, "I'd get up and take her on walks. We'd go to the store. If I'm down and out, I'll pet her and I'll feel better. She's a big ol' lovable dog. We call her the big teddy bear."

She and Bella take life day by day. While radiation has kept the tumor from growing and a human attendant helps Adams, Roquemore believes Bella has played a major role.

"Bella is an exceptional dog," said Dr. Violet Shen of the Children's Hospital of Orange County, Calif. "She accompanied Heather to all her doctor's appointments and has provided great emotional support and companionship to Heather."

The calm, gentle-spirited dog puts her Retriever instincts to good use, grabbing the phone and picking up carrots or anything else Adams happens to drop. When she is sick in bed, Bella snuggles up and lays her head on Adams' chest. When she falls, the dog stands firm to support Adams as she lifts herself up.

Perhaps most important is the independence Bella engenders. Adams rides an electric cart in stores while Bella grabs items from a shelf.

When Adams goes to doctor appointments at clinics, she makes a point of stopping in the pediatric area, where kids fawn over the dog, and Bella wiggles with attitude. When the pair go to friends' homes, Bella sneaks her way into bedrooms to grab a stuffed animal, returning to present it as if to say: "Look what I found."

Adams, ever grateful for the dog, sends cards and notes to Roquemore to update her on her former companion. Meanwhile, Roquemore has acquired a new service dog—Noble, another Golden Retriever. "I went without a dog for about two years," Roquemore said, who occasionally visits Bella. "It was difficult."

"This dog is phenomenal," Murray said. "You don't even have to call or motion her to come; she just goes. She's totally dedicated to her."

from DOG FANCY

A Full Partner

DONNA BOETIG

---

*E*very time 33-year-old California attorney Natalie Wormeli went on a job interview, she cringed. Wormeli, who graduated from the University of California, Davis, Law School in 1993, is blind and wheelchair-bound from multiple sclerosis. No matter how hard she tried, her confidence vanished when her husband, Ben, had to wheel her into an office to meet a prospective employer.

After a few attempts to find work, she retreated to her home to practice law. Her clients were referrals from friends. "I settled many cases from bed," she says. Still, Wormeli missed being with colleagues.

Then, in September 1996, she received her ticket to freedom: Bruno. The three-year-old, 95-pound Labrador retriever is the only dog in the country who's trained to serve his owner as both eyes and limbs.

Bruno came from Paws With a Cause, a nonprofit group that trains assistance dogs for the disabled. He lived for 18 months with a foster family, who taught him basic manners. Next, Mike Sapp, founder of Paws, spent a year training Bruno to perform basic seeing-eye-dog duties and service tasks, like flipping a light switch and picking up change.

Then came the real test: Bruno was delivered to Wormeli.

Within weeks he was directing her on and off buses and nav-
igating her across busy streets. Thanks to Bruno, this past
summer Wormeli landed a three-month contract to work for a
nonprofit legal-advocacy group in Sacramento. Each weekday
morning from June through August, Wormeli's husband drove
the duo a half hour to her office. There, Bruno opened the outside doors, pressed the elevator button to Wormeli's floor, then
settled down beside her for a morning of work. By afternoon,
Wormeli says, "my office would become a petting zoo."

Wormeli, now back to practicing law from her house, is
looking for another full-time job. But the prospect is no longer
frightening: "Bruno makes me feel more optimistic about in-
terviews," she says. Not to mention the extra incentive he gives
her to find another position: "Bruno," Wormeli adds, "really
misses going to the office."

from McCALL'S

Rare Gifts

CHRISTIANE LAVIN

$\mathcal{A}$s an intravenous needle slides into Rowdy's jugular vein and begins to draw blood, W. Jean Dodds, D.V.M., hugs him tightly and whispers a few soothing words. But if the happy-go-lucky greyhound is fazed by the four-minute procedure, he doesn't show it. "He knows a treat is coming," says Dodds, laughing. And judging by the frantic action of his tail as he scarfs down the canine cookie, his reward was well worth the donation.

Rowdy is one of about 135 greyhounds—all former racing dogs—living at Hemopet blood bank in Irving, CA, while donating blood to help sick canines. "This is more or less a Red Cross for dogs," explains Dodds, who opened Hemopet in 1991. Thanks to her initiative, countless canines in need of hip replacement, bypass surgery, and other lifesaving procedures can count on healthy, compatible blood transfusions. Shipments are sent out daily around the United States and as far away as Japan.

Dodds, 57, recalls being struck with the idea for Hemopet: "It dawned on me: Dogs have accidents and illnesses the same way people do, and to be properly treated, they also need a safe supply of blood." Within five years, armed with $250,000 from grants, individual donations, and money Dodds earned from lecturing, Hemopet became a reality. It's now one of four animal blood banks in the United States, and the only one that's nonprofit.

But Dodd's mission goes beyond safe transfusions. The adoption branch of Hemopet, called Pet Life-Line, finds loving homes for greyhound donors who would otherwise have been euthanized after their racing days were over. "Once they can no longer win, they're out of luck," Dodds explains. "It's tragic."

She's screened about 1,200 greyhounds to date. Those with an untainted, universal blood type—about 20 percent—join Hemopet; the rest are placed with adoptive families. Doggie donors live at Hemopet for about a year and a half before they, too, are adopted.

Dodds, a lifelong animal lover ("I signed up for veterinary school the second I could"), doesn't run the bank alone— there are 23 employees and 50 volunteers on hand to help. Besides feeding, grooming, and walking the dogs, the Hemopet crew provides companionship. "We teach the dogs that it's okay to cut loose and play," says senior volunteer Toni Bryant. "We keep 'em hoppin'." Dodd's husband, patent attorney and fellow pooch lover Charles Berman, helps out too.

Dodds encourages families hoping to adopt to drop by on several occasions for some pet bonding time. "But," she explains, "we're a little choosy." She's not kidding. Candidates must own their own home or have written proof that their landlord allows pets, have a fenced-in yard, complete a five-page application, and even present letters of recommendation. One recent applicant—a former police officer—didn't cut it. "He wanted a macho dog. I told him, 'A greyhound's too soft and gentle for you.' He was fuming, but we sent him away."

Despite such high standards, just about every one of the

dogs eventually finds a home—even the "ugly muglies." That's what Dodds lovingly calls the slightly homely canines. And if it should happen that there's a pooch no one wants? "Then he has a home with us for life," she says.

from GOOD HOUSEKEEPING

Melissa and Mindy

PENNY BARGO

---

*D*eafness is a characteristic weakness in the Dalmatian breed, but that fact was far from my mind as I filled aluminum pans with puppy food, and tickled the ears of several frisky Dalmatian pups tugging at an old sock. This was the fourth litter of puppies I'd cared for, and I felt a lot more confident than I had with the first. When those first puppies were born without spots, I'd thought the litter was faulty. I didn't know that all Dals are pure white at birth.

Breeding Dalmatians was not a business for me—it was a ministry. The "Kennels for Christ" started in 1980, when my son presented me with a pair of Dalmatians as a gift. He knew I'd longed for a Dalmatian since childhood. But I'd never really expected to own one, much less two.

Having the handsome pair in my possession turned my thoughts in another direction. Why couldn't I begin a "puppy ministry" to raise money for the missionary couple I'd been helping to support in the Lucknow area of India for several years?

We purchased kennel fencing and poured concrete for the runs, and the Lord even saw to it that I got another pair of Dalmatians from the same strain. We were on our way!

The Dals were cooperative enough and bred according to schedule—every other season, for health's sake. Three litters of pouncing pups resulted in a few thousand dollars for my missionary friends. The present litter of seven were particularly well-marked pups, promising another thousand. They were a quiet litter, however, and often when I entered the puppy room, several pups would not wake up until trampled upon by their rambunctious siblings. As usual I had no trouble selling them.

I had just mailed the missionaries' check when the first call came:

"We noticed that the puppy didn't respond when we called her, so we took her to the veterinarian, and he told us she seems to be deaf . . . "

It was the first of three such calls. I refunded the already-spent money and took the puppies back, except for one. Maggie's owner had gotten so attached that she wanted to keep her; even so, I returned her money too.

Most Dalmatian breeders have deaf puppies put to sleep. I just couldn't handle that. Now that Melissa and Mindy were in my home (and under my feet) again, they had invaded my affections.

But they also managed other invasions, and my household became a disaster area. One day I returned home to find that the pair had chewed their way through the wire-mesh barrier that blocked the doorway to the "romper room." I had only to follow the puddles and plops to locate the rascals. They were in the living room, ecstatically chewing on a leg of the piano bench. The floor lamp was lying across the upset coffee table. The lamp shade was crushed, with brown paw prints spattered upon it. They had even managed to chew through the stereo cord without getting electrocuted. Of course, they were oblivious to my yelling and scolding because they couldn't hear.

On another occasion, I found Melissa inside the cupboard

under the kitchen sink, scampering through the spilled detergent. Mindy was under the table demolishing my new sponge mop. When they eventually noticed my arrival, it wasn't with a sense of guilt, but with leg-lapping, clambering, tail-wagging greetings, after which they flopped at my feet, exhausted from wickedness.

What to do with these lovable little sinners? I couldn't afford to keep two more puppies as well as the two pairs of breeders, along with Beau, an eight-month-old pup I had kept from a previous litter. The situation looked grim.

"Lord," I prayed, "You know how I feel about these pups. I doubt there is any way to save them, but if You know one, please show me."

Several days later I took Beau outside to drill him on his obedience training. He circled around the yard at my left heel, with Melissa and Mindy somersaulting behind. When I stopped, Beau took his cue, stopped and sat as he had been trained. The pups sat too, and watched expectantly. I gave Beau the hand signal to "stay," and I walked away. When I turned around the pups were still sitting there with Beau. "Come," I commanded, giving the accompanying signal. Beau walked to me, the pups romping behind. The pups followed Beau everywhere, and I was learning to get their attention through him.

About a week later, as I prepared the puppy food, the spotted twins were jumping and pawing at my legs. My thoughts were preoccupied, and even though Beau was not there, I gave the hand signal to "sit." Both pups immediately sat. I was astonished. Was it just a coincidence? Testing, I gave the signal for "stay" and took several steps across the kitchen. They wagged their tails and danced with excitement on their rumps, *but they stayed.* "Come," I signaled, and they bounded to me! I gathered the frolicking pair into my arms and cried as their tongues lapped my face.

That did it! God had shown me a way. Melissa and Mindy were not only healthy, frisky pups, but they were trainable too. All they needed now was a sheltered environment, and somehow I would find it.

The puppies were almost three months old when I wrote letters to the editors of two local newspapers. I described my spotted friends and the dilemma their handicap posed, and appealed for appropriate homes. The next day two reporters arrived, cameras in hand. Each of the newspapers ran the story of Melissa and Mindy with an urgent appeal for the special kind of protective care they required—a home away from traffic with a patient, loving owner willing to learn new communication skills. Melissa and Mindy were offered free to the right homes.

As soon as the story appeared, I was flooded with calls. One after another, concerned people offered their homes to Melissa and Mindy, until *70* candidates had responded to the appeal! It was difficult to screen and select the homes where Melissa and Mindy would live, for each phone call came from a sincere dog lover, but eventually I chose two. Although I was attached to the pups by this time, parting with them was comparatively easy because they now had a future. That gave me reason enough to smile, but there was another reason too.

I hadn't been able to imagine how God would rescue Mindy and Melissa. He did it by giving them one of their own kind to set an example—the same as He did for us 2,000 years ago.

When God Closes a Door

VERA SCARANGELLO

---

*Q*uietly I entered the bedroom with Sugar, my beloved guide dog, at my side. She'd been with me for 10 of the 25 years I'd been blind. My husband was asleep. Gently I laid a hand on his shoulder; a lump formed in my throat as I felt his skeletal frame.

"Only a matter of months now," the doctor had said. The hall clock chimed; it was 5:00 A.M. Sugar pushed against my leg. Time to catch the bus for work. I lingered another precious minute. We'd been married 32 years, and we fit together like our names—Vera and Vito. We had planned to grow old together.

Another nudge from Sugar. "Okay, old girl," I said, reaching for the leather handle of her harness. In my coat pocket was a biscuit, a reward for her struggling down two steep flights of steps. Every day my life was entrusted to this 65-pound yellow Labrador retriever, and not once had she let me down.

"She shouldn't put in another winter," my father, who lived downstairs, said. I prayed he was wrong. I couldn't lose her and Vito at the same time. When I got her from Guiding Eyes for the Blind, I was told that the working life of such dogs is from 8 to 10 years. Then they must be retired.

Not now, Jesus, I begged. *Give her strength till after Vito…
till I've had time to grieve for him.*

Sugar and I persevered down the stairs. *She's not as bad as
she seems,* I rationalized. *Just early morning stiffness, is all.* At
the bottom I handed her a biscuit and praised her. She accepted both with quiet dignity. Then her nose was to the door.
Nothing turned her from her duty.

Outside, in the autumn-spiced air, damp leaves swirled
around my ankles. I pulled my coat tighter, feeling all too
keenly the coming winter. *"Vito,"* my heart cried. We crossed
the street, Sugar and I, to the bus stop. Soon we heard the
grind and hiss of the bus as it pulled to the curb. The driver
lowered the steps and we got on.

I took my usual seat near the front. Sugar crawled underneath and snoozed. From Fort Hamilton in Brooklyn, it is a
45-minute ride into Manhattan, with one bus change between.
I settled back.

I'd gone blind at 27 from retinitis pigmentosa, diagnosed
when I was 12. It was hard—but not the end of the world, really. Many blind people never see at all. I'd seen everything that
was important to me, including all four of our children.

I was blessed with a good memory and organizational
skills that helped me cope. And I had Vito. Vito loved to talk.
His language was beautiful. With his words, he made me see!

In August 1988 Vito had gone to the doctor with a sore
throat. The lab report came back with a death sentence. Vito,
who never ran out of words, was silent. I put my hand up to his
face and felt his jaw, stiff with shock and anger.

His voice box had to be taken out. After the operation, we
communicated through a voice synthesizer. Vito loved people,
but many pulled away from him because of the robot-like way

he talked. Three anguished years passed and we were on the edge of winter 1991. Heavily medicated for pain, Vito slept most of the time. Every day I wept—for myself and for what Vito was going through. Then would come the sweet lull of God's whisper, promising never to leave me and not to put more on Vito than he could bear. *Trust Me,* God seemed to say. *Even now.*

But now it was Sugar. Her old age, with its aches and stiffness, came suddenly. Could I really trust God?

The bus was almost full, and we chugged along heavily. Regulars got on and greeted me, petting Sugar and asking about Vito. I smiled and answered. But inside I felt tormented. Was it fair to ask this dog—who'd given so much and would still give more if I asked—to go on? I reached down and patted her head. Her ears perked. I knew I had to give her up. But I was angry. *Why now, Jesus?*

I thought back to another time, another trial. Ever since I was a child and had visited FBI headquarters on a tour to Washington, D.C., my blood raced at the thought of being part of this organization. But at 19 I was told they did not accept anyone with vision problems. I wanted to scream at the unfairness, for my vision was still good.

So I got a job as a laboratory technician at St. Vincent's Hospital in Manhattan. And met Vito. He was a patient, and I was sent to do some blood work on him. My parents had given me a beautiful diamond for my birthday, and I was wearing it. "That's some gizmo on your finger," he said as I arranged the glass tubes in my kit. "Who's the lucky guy?" I started to make up a name just to brush him off. Then I looked at him . . . at those dark, romantic eyes . . . and stammered the truth.

Six months later we were married. That I would someday

be blind bothered him not at all. "Now I know why God gave me this gift of gab," he said. "I'll be your eyes." We had four children close together, three girls and a boy. I treasured every glimpse of them.

When my children were older, I began to get restless around the house, though, by then, I couldn't see. "I'd like to go back to work," I told Vito. "Sounds good," he said.

A few days later I turned on the radio to hear an announcement that the FBI was now recruiting the disabled—even the blind. I felt a rush of excitement. All I had to do was learn word processing at the Lighthouse run by the New York Association for the Blind. I hadn't a doubt that I would be accepted now. I applied and passed the test and interview with flying colors.

My one dread was going to work with a cane. "Isn't there another way, Lord?" I asked.

Vito dropped me off for my first day of training, and I clumsily made my way inside with my cane. Tapping into a room full of people, I almost stepped on a guide dog named Webster. When I leaned down to make my apologies, his owner was touched and insisted I try him. It was magic. I couldn't wait to tell Vito.

"Oh, Vito," I said that evening, "I felt so grand walking with Webster. I walked with my head up, my shoulders back!" There was a catch in Vito's voice as he said, "Then let's get a Webster for you." I hugged him tight.

Two months later I was standing nervously in the hall at Guiding Eyes for the Blind in Yorktown Heights, New York, leash in hand. I was about to meet Sugar. I heard a door open. "Vera, call your dog," a trainer said. "Sugar, come," I said. *Pad, pad, pad.* A cold nose pressed my arm. I ran my hands over her sleek body. She was shivering. I put my arms around her, speaking softly. I was already beginning to love her. When I left the center a month later, I had an independence that had not been mine since I went blind. And I had a friend whose devotion was total.

On September 28, 1981, with Sugar leading the way, I walked into the Federal Building in Manhattan to start my new job with the FBI. I loved it. Sugar stayed by my desk. Everyone adored her, both at work and home, though she was not an openly affectionate dog. "Do you love me, Sugar?" I'd ask, putting my arms around her. I'd feel her nose go in the air as if to say, "How can you ask? Don't I show it every day?"

With the kids leaving home, Vito and I grew even closer. We explored the city together, Vito narrating. We ate at our favorite restaurants, Vito lovingly reciting the menus. Those were beautiful years . . .

My bus driver jolted me back to the present. "Vera, here's your stop." Sugar took me to where the Number 27 express bus to Manhattan would pick us up. I smelled the salty tang of the East River and heard the plaintive cry of the gulls. "Oh, Sugar, how will I live without you?"

Guiding Eyes would send her to a good home. And she would adjust well. Adjustment had been a part of her breeding. But what about me?

They came for her on a rainy Saturday. I hugged her neck, weeping, while she stood still, head down, tail low. I waited outside my door, listening to her hobble down the steps one last time. The door to the apartment house opened and closed. She was gone. I went to the bedroom and sat beside Vito. He was crying. In all our years of marriage I had never known him to cry.

I missed Sugar dreadfully and wondered how I would ever

adjust to another dog. Even in the best of times it's difficult. I was apprehensive when Geoff, from Guiding Eyes, called me at work. "We have a special dog for you. It seems so right that he came in from training now. His name is York. I must warn you, though, he's not a Sugar dog."

The Guiding Eyes van came to me early in December, during the first cold snap. I stood at the top of the steps and heard 85 pounds of black Labrador enthusiasm thumping up toward me. Two enormous paws landed on my shoulders. York was licking my face! Geoff stood by quietly.

"He shows his feelings, doesn't he?" I said, laughing.

"Yes, and so do you," Geoff said.

When we walked, York was as smooth as a carousel horse and oozed confidence that was catching. It took about four steps for us to click and become a team—almost unheard of.

One night not long afterward, I sat in the living room, alone with my new dog. Vito was in the hospital. He was leaving me fast. I began sobbing. Suddenly York was on the sofa beside me, his big head on my shoulder. I reached out and burrowed my face against him, feeling comforted for the first time in months. "Thank you, Jesus," I prayed, "for sending me York."

Vito died the day after Valentine's. I was with him when he took his last breath, like a relieved sigh. At the funeral, when York left my side, my daughter whispered that he was sitting like a sentry at Vito's casket. At the end of the service he came back and put his head in my lap.

Jesus said, "I will not leave you comfortless. I will come to you" (John 14:18). He does—in quiet moments within me, in family, friends and, yes, in a big black Lab who came when I needed him most.

After the funeral I remembered how awful I thought surrendering Sugar had been. The timing had seemed so cruel. But God had meant it for my good, just as he had in all the events of my life.

God's timing is never wrong, not even by a hair.

Feathered Friend

JO COUDERT

"**I**'m going nuts here by myself," Pat Myers confessed to her daughter, Annie. Pat had been virtually confined to her house for a year as she was treated for an inflamed artery in her temple that affected her vision and stamina.

A widow with two married children, she'd been happily running a chain of dress shops. But now that she had to give up her business, her home began to feel oppressively silent and empty. Finally she admitted to Annie how lonely she was.

"Do you think I should advertise for someone to live with me?"

"That's such a gamble," Annie said. "How about a pet?"

"I haven't the strength to walk a dog," Pat said. "I'm allergic to cats, and fish don't have a whole lot to say."

"Birds do," said her daughter. "Why not get a parrot?" And so it began.

Pat and Annie visited a breeder of African Greys and were shown two little featherless creatures huddled together for warmth. Pat was doubtful, but Annie persuaded her to put a deposit down on the bird with the bright eyes. When he was three months old and feathered out, he was delivered to his new owner, who named him Casey.

A few weeks later Pat told Annie, "I didn't realize I talked so much. Casey's picking up all kinds of words."

"I told you." Her daughter smiled at the sound of pleasure in Pat's voice.

The first sentence Casey learned was "Where's my glasses?" followed by "Where's my purse?" Whenever Pat began scanning tabletops and opening drawers, Casey chanted, "Where's my glasses? Where's my purse?" When she returned from an errand, he'd greet her with, "Holy smokes, it's cold out there," in a perfect imitation of her voice.

Casey disliked being caged, so Pat often let him roam the house. "What fun it is to have him," she told Annie. "It makes the whole place feel better."

"I think *you're* beginning to feel better too," said Annie.

"Well, he gives me four or five laughs a day—they say laughter's good for you."

Once a plumber came to repair a leak under the kitchen sink. In the den, Casey cracked seeds in his cage and eyed the plumber through the open door. Suddenly the parrot broke the silence, reciting, "One potato, two potato, three potato, four . . ."

"What?" asked the plumber.

"Don't poo on the rug," Casey ordered, in Pat's voice.

The plumber pushed himself out from under the sink and marched to the living room. "If you're going to play games, lady, you can just get yourself another plumber." Pat looked at him blankly. The plumber hesitated, "That was you, wasn't it?"

Pat smiled. "What was me?"

"One potato, two potato—and don't poo on the rug."

"Oh, dear," said Pat. "Let me introduce you to Casey."

Casey saw them coming. "What's going on around here?" he said.

At that moment Pat sneezed. Casey immediately mimicked the sneeze, added a couple of Pat's coughs at her allergic worst and finished with Pat's version of "Wow!" The plumber shook his head slowly and crawled back under the sink.

One morning while Pat was reading the paper, the phone rang. She picked it up and got a dial tone. The next morning it rang again, and again she got a dial tone. The third morning she realized what was going on: Casey had learned to mimic the phone faultlessly.

Once, as Pat opened a soda can at the kitchen table, Casey waddled over and snatched at the can. It toppled, sending a cascade of cola onto her lap and the floor. "*#@!" Pat said. Casey eyed her. "Forget you heard that," she ordered. "I didn't say it. I never say it. And I wouldn't have now if I hadn't just mopped the floor." Casey kept his beak shut.

Later a real-estate agent arrived to go over some business. She and Pat were deep in discussion when Casey screamed from the den, "*#@!"

Both women acted as though they'd heard nothing.

Liking the sibilance, Casey tried it again. "*#@!" he said. And again. "*#@! *#@! *#@!"

Caught between humiliation and amusement, Pat put her hand on her guest's arm. "Helen, it's sweet of you to pretend, but I know you haven't suddenly gone deaf." They both broke up laughing.

"Oh, you bad bird," Pat scolded after the agent left. "She's going to think I go around all day saying four-letter words."

"What a mess," Casey said.

"You're darned right," Pat told him.

Casey's favorite perch in the kitchen was the faucet in the sink; his favorite occupation, trying to remove the washer at the end of it. Once, to tease him, Pat sprinkled a handful of water over him. Casey ceased his attack on the washer and swiveled his head to look at her sharply. "What's the matter with you?" he demanded.

If he left the kitchen and Pat heard him say "Oh, you bad bird!" she knew to come running. Casey was either pecking at her dining room chairs or the wallpaper in the foyer.

"Is it worth it?" her son, Bill, asked, looking at the damaged front hall.

"Give me a choice between a perfect, lonely house and a tacky, happy one," said Pat, "and I'll take the tacky one any day."

But Pat did decide to have Casey's sharp claws clipped. To trim them without getting bitten, the vet wrapped Casey tightly in a towel, turned him on his back and handed him to an assistant to hold while he went to work. A helpless Casey looked at Pat and said piteously, "Oh, the poor baby."

Pat often wondered if Casey knew what he was saying. Sometimes the statements were so appropriate she couldn't be sure. Like the time a guest had lingered on and on talking in the doorway and Casey finally called out impatiently, "Night, night."

Yet, whenever Pat wanted to teach him something, Casey could be maddening. Once she carried him to the living room and settled in an easy chair as Casey sidled up her arm and nestled his head against her chest. Pat dusted the tips of her fingers over his velvet-gray feathers and scarlet tail. "I love you," she said. "Can you say, 'I love you, Pat Myers?'"

Casey cocked an eye at her. "I live on Mallard View," he said.

"I know where you live, funny bird. Tell me you love me."

"Funny bird."

Another time Pat was trying to teach Casey "Jingle Bell

Rock" before her children and grandchildren arrived for Christmas dinner. "It'll be your contribution," she told him.

"Where's my glasses?"

"Never mind that. Just listen to me sing." But as Pat sang "Jingle bell, jingle bell, jingle bell rock" and danced around the kitchen, Casey simply looked at her.

Finally Pat gave up. And all through Christmas dinner Casey was silent. When it came time for dessert, Pat extinguished the lights and touched a match to the plum pudding. As the brandy blazed up, with impeccable timing Casey burst into "Jingle bell, jingle bell, jingle bell rock!"

Pat's health improved so much she decided to go on a three-week vacation. "You'll be all right," she told Casey. "You can stay with Annie and the kids."

The day her mother was due back, Annie returned Casey to the apartment so he'd be there when Pat got home from the airport.

"Hi, Casey!" Pat called as she unlocked the door. There was no answer. "Holy smokes, it's cold out there!" she said. More silence. Pat dropped her coat and hurried into the den. Casey glared at her.

"Hey, aren't you glad to see me?" The bird moved to the far side of the cage. "Come on, don't be angry," Pat said. She opened the door of the cage and held out her hand. Casey dropped to the bottom of the cage and huddled there.

In the morning Pat tried again. Casey refused to speak. Later that day he consented to climb on her wrist and be carried to the living room. When she sat down, he shifted uneasily and seemed about to fly away. "Please, Casey," Pat pleaded, "I know I was away a long time, but you've got to forgive me."

Casey took a few tentative steps up her arm, then moved

back to her knee. "Were you afraid I was never going to come back?" she said softly. "I would never do that."

Casey cocked his head and slowly moved up her arm. Pat crooked her elbow, and Casey nestled against her. Pat stroked his head, smoothing his feathers with her forefinger. Finally Casey spoke.

"I love you, Pat Myers," he said.

from READER'S DIGEST

SUPER SLEUTHS

*"To get a grip on a job that's waiting,
dig in with determination."*

NIKI ANDERSON

It's no mystery—animals, particularly dogs, are valued members of our law enforcement agencies. They not only prevent crimes but help to identify and find people who commit them. And, as any of their handlers will tell you, they're great partners. They're good company, they take pride in their work, and if you need protection, you don't even have to ask for it.

Not all the animals who keep us safe are trained for police work. Some of them are our loving, devoted family pets who at this moment might be curled up in a chair by the fireplace.

"Which Way, Bruno?"

SHERRY BENNETT WARSHAUER

In January of 1995, an East Hartford, Connecticut, police officer named William Proulx pulled a car over to the side of the road. The driver had been driving erratically and had nearly struck Proulx's cruiser. He was apparently intoxicated or on drugs. The license plate check revealed that the car was stolen. During a routine stop, Proulx's dog, Bruno, is trained to hang out the window. His bark can be a great deterrent. The officer approached the car and asked the subject to step out of the car. He refused. Officer Proulx opened the driver's door and reached in to grab the keys. The driver put the car in gear and accelerated, dragging Proulx onto the on-ramp of the highway as he held precariously to the driver and steering wheel. Officer Proulx had not called Bruno, fearing that the dog would be run over. However, Bruno realized Proulx was in trouble. He correctly perceived an attack upon his partner and responded without being commanded, an instinctive reaction. His 80-pound frame moved with lightning speed. A few seconds later, he was sitting in the passenger seat with the driver's arm secured in his mouth, restraining him long enough for the officer to gain control of the situation. The only door that gave access to the inside of the car was the driver's side. Bruno must have run after the car and jumped over Proulx's back in order to enter the car.

Once again, he saved the day. Since May of 1994, the team of Bruno, a black-and-tan German Shepherd Dog acquired from Guiding Eyes for the Blind, and Officer William Proulx has made 190 felony arrests.

Bruno was raised to become a guide dog. In his early weeks of training, though, it was apparent that he was too distracted by other dogs to be a reliable guide dog. Due to his excellent tracking and defensing skills, Guiding Eyes for the Blind had him trained to do police work. Because many people are afraid of them, dogs are often successful as deterrents. Officer Proulx claims that if a suspect is running away from the scene of a crime, he will yell out that he has a dog, which usually makes the suspect stop, knowing that he or she will be chased down. Bruno has helped Proulx stop fights that would normally have taken a dozen officers to control—nobody wants to tangle with a police dog. If a perpetrator is beyond Bruno's reach—in a closet, attic or other hiding place—Bruno will guard the spot and bark for Officer Proulx.

Most dogs used for police work are male German Shepherd Dogs. They are well-suited for police work because they are extremely loyal, they are large, they are fast and they can be fierce and intimidating. They have a fabulous ability to follow a scent and are inquisitive and aggressive. They can tolerate the extremes of hot and cold weather, and they ride well in cars. Proulx says, "The mistake you make is when you don't trust your dog's instinct. You will arrive at a scene where everyone is pointing to the man who ran southbound, and the dog wants to go northbound. The experienced officer will go north." Patrol dogs are continuously kept in training to hone their skills. On a slow night, Officer Proulx will have another officer go to a field and climb a tree. This second officer, playing the part of a perpetrator, will encourage Bruno to use his incredible tracking skills to locate him. Bruno gets excited and starts to whine when he begins these games. He loves the sport and loves to win.

He is trained to attack a party on command, and he will also instinctively defend the officer, even without command. The dog is trained to act on his own instinct, particularly in the event that the officer is incapacitated. Bruno's tasks also include evidence recovery. He has found many weapons near crime scenes. On an evening in September of 1994, Officer Proulx was assigned to investigate a report of "vandalism" to a motel room in East Hartford. Officer Proulx, hampered in communicating with the motel manager at the scene due to a language barrier, deciphered that a male with a gun had been seen in the area. He had actually been shooting a gun out of a motel window. Officer Proulx and Bruno stepped outside of the motel office into the darkness. The officer was confronted by a fully loaded semi-automatic pistol no more than 15 feet away held with a two-handed combat grip and pointed at his chest. The perpetrator had been hiding in the shadow of the shrubbery. The surge of adrenaline was accompanied by the immediate reaction of the officer and K-9 team, who were using skills honed by training and experience. Bruno attacked the subject, causing him to turn away from Proulx. In an instant the officer's gun was drawn. Once the perpetrator was cornered, he surrendered. He had been high on crack and cocaine, and he was a deadly threat. His weapon, a 9mm Browning, fully loaded with Winchester silvertip hollow points (known as flesh-destroying ammunition), was cocked and ready to fire. There is no doubt that Bruno's dedication, loyalty and immediate response saved Officer Proulx's life that night.

Proulx's leadership and bravery and Bruno's faithful actions are worthy of the highest praise and commendation.

Satisfaction for Bruno can be translated into responding to "code 3" calls and catching the "bad guys." He likes nothing better than when Officer Proulx grabs his tracking harness and they pile into the patrol car and speed with the sirens wailing and lights flashing to their next assignment. Proulx can't help but feel that Bruno wants to push him to go faster or maybe wants to drive the car himself.

In one incident, a stolen jeep had hit a pedestrian and flipped over. By the time Proulx and Bruno arrived, the police at the scene had three people in custody. They were searching a swamp for the final suspect. Too many officers in the swamp confused the scents. Bruno, however, picked up on a sweat-produced chemical, apocrine, which is emitted when a human being is frightened. It cannot be simulated. A K-9 can go through crowds of people to select the person emitting the apocrine. Bruno found the suspect and cornered him until Proulx took over.

Tracking or searching for a subject by following a scent is second nature to Bruno. To Bruno, tracking is a game. He is rewarded immediately after successfully achieving his task. "Good boy" in an enthusiastic, high-pitched voice and a game of retrieving a stick is Bruno's favorite gratification.

Once the team was called to a break-in at a residence. Officer Proulx brought Bruno in harness around the back of the house. Bruno went tracking through the neighborhood. The weather conditions were ideal; Bruno tracked right back to the house. The other officers assured Proulx that they had checked the house and surrounding area thoroughly, finding nothing. Bruno persisted by constantly tracking back to a tree in the front yard. A group of officers, who had been milling around below the tree, were duly impressed and somewhat embarrassed when they looked up and saw the suspect.

In another case, a woman with Alzheimer's disease was reported missing by her husband. Using the woman's jacket for a scent, Officer Proulx and Bruno searched the neighborhood for more than an hour before finding the woman sitting in a neighbor's car, about a ¼-mile from her house. The woman was slouched in the seat and could not be seen from the outside. Bruno indicated she was in the car by scratching at the car door. . . .

This successful team loves to get out there and fight crime. Bruno is in his prime and can look forward to many successful years ahead. When he retires, he will become the Proulx family pet.

Proulx is married and has two young children and Bruno is very much a family member. When he comes running toward you with his large black face and body and thundering paws, you hold your breath, with no way of knowing that he will come to a screeching halt and roll over.

from EVERYDAY HEROES

The Nose Knows Best

VIRGINIA PHELPS CLEMENS

"There's a bomb on Continental Flight 608," said the harsh-sounding voice on the other end of the line. Then, click, the caller hung up.

The airport official replaced his receiver and paused for a second before making a call to Officer Jim Manning.

"Jim, I just received an anonymous phone call. We have a bomb scare on Continental 608," he said quickly. "Get Alex down to the end of Runway 6. I'll call the pilot of the plane and tell him to turn around and meet us there."

Runway 6 was the farthest runway from the terminal building. By the time the airport official got there, Continental Flight 608 had already arrived and opened its doors. The passengers were beginning to file off, carrying their coats and any small packages they had brought on the plane themselves. Their luggage was being unloaded from the cargo hold by the loading crew.

Officer Manning stood patiently nearby with Alex, a large black-and-tan German shepherd, sitting at his left side.

Finally all the passengers had left the plane.

"O.K. I'm taking Alex inside now. Please keep everyone

out. I'll be ready to search the luggage in a few minutes," Officer Manning told the airport official. "Have the bomb crew ready in case he finds something."

The young man quickly climbed the portable stairs and entered the plane. Alex trotted happily at his heel. He knew he was going to be able to play the game soon.

Inside the plane, Officer Manning unsnapped the leash and said, "O.K., Alex, find the bomb."

Eagerly, the dog trotted down the aisle, sniffing at each seat. Tail wagging, ears pricked forward, and nose drawing in the various smells, Alex searched for "that scent." This was a game he loved to play. Unfortunately, he couldn't always find "the scent." Sometimes it wasn't where Officer Manning sent him to hunt for it.

After making a complete tour of the plane, including the cockpit, galley (kitchen), and rest rooms, the shepherd trotted back to Officer Manning and sat down in front of him. Disappointment showed in every line of his body from his drooping tail to his limp ears and low-hung head.

"That's all right, Alex. We're not finished yet."

Officer Manning patted him sympathetically and snapped the leash onto his collar. Then together they searched the passenger cabin again. This time Officer Manning went with Alex, pointed to various areas, and said, "Is it there? Find it! Find the bomb, Alex."

But they found nothing unusual inside the plane.

Outside again, the partners walked over to where the luggage had been placed in a long line down the runway, five feet between each piece.

"Everyone stand back, please," Officer Manning said to the small group of men nearby.

"Give him room to work."

Turning to the dog sitting at his side, he unsnapped the leash again and commanded, "Alex, find the bomb!"

Alex bounded forward, ears erect and nose already exploring the air currents. At the first piece of luggage he slowed his pace, gave a sniff, and continued on down the line, barely turning his head at most of the suitcases.

Suddenly, he stopped in mid-stride and turned toward a dark-brown briefcase.

"Alex, heel!"

The dog whirled and returned quickly to his partner. Disgust showed all over his face. That was it. He knew "the scent" was in there and he wanted to get at it.

"That's it," said Officer Manning to the other men standing behind him. "The brown briefcase."

"Are you sure?" asked one of them in disbelief.

"Yes, let the bomb crew handle it now." He bent down and patted the dog heartily.

"Good boy, Alex. I knew you could find it. Good boy."

In spite of his disappointment at not being able to retrieve "the scent" and play with it, Alex's eyes brightened and his body wriggled with joy at his partner's praise.

As the bomb crew moved in to take possession of the suspected case, Officer Manning walked back toward the terminal building. Alex followed at his side, head held high and tail wagging happily with every step. He had performed his job perfectly, saving hours and possibly lives with his nose.

from SUPER ANIMALS AND THEIR UNUSUAL CAREERS

Requiem for a Junkyard Dog

DAN NEIL

---

*B*ill Dierker doesn't lock up at night. Which at first might seem odd. After all, Dierker's garage—British Automotive Specialists in Peoria, Illinois—is in the middle of a rusty and decomposing landscape of scrap yards, rail yards, and factories so squalid it's practically radioactive. Dierker's 160-by-160-foot lot, surrounded by chain-link fence, is "in the heart of the wine country," he says. On a clear day he can hear the gunfire.

And yet he fears no evil. For Dierker has Ned, the biggest, baddest junkyard dog in the valley. If not the world. Weighing a girthy and ill-tempered 251 pounds, Ned is a mixed breed of Great Dane, Saint Bernard, and Buick.

His veterinarian, Dr. Scott Demanes, describes Ned's head as the size of a "microwave oven."

Now a ripe old 14 years—very ripe, by all accounts—Ned is gray in the muzzle, overweight, with a touch of arthritis. He has lost a couple steps on his hole shot toward the fence. "We use him mainly as a deterrent," says Dierker. "He doesn't have to do much but growl."

As the "Director of Security Operations," Ned leaves most of the chasing and barking to the six younger dogs under him. They include an epileptic Irish setter named Fitz and a Chinese Shar-Pei-English bulldog mix. The dogs hang out in Ned's private office, the only heated and air-conditioned room in the garage.

But woe betide the burglar who underestimates Ned, says Dr. Dave Harvey, an emergency-medicine physician who is friends with Dierker. "I've seen Ned get angry, and it's quite impressive. He takes his guard-dog duties very seriously."

Ned's legend began 12 years ago at another junkyard after he badly damaged an employee there. The victim, a prisoner working on a furlough program, had been spitefully spraying Ned with a water hose. "Ned hates to be sprayed with water," Dierker notes absolvingly. Ned backed up into his doghouse until the offending trustee got within striking distance. Then Ned charged him and nearly bit his arm *off*.

"Ned broke both the bones—the radius and the ulna—in the guy's arm and did all this nerve damage," Dierker recalls. The prisoner had to have his arm put back together with metal plates. In 16 years of trauma medicine, Dr. Harvey has never seen a major "crush injury" from a dog bite.

Bad dog! Down, boy!

That junkyard went out of business, and Dierker inherited Ned, along with a doghouse, some tools, and a rusty '79 Toyota. "All's gone by the wayside but Ned," says Dierker.

Since then, Ned has faithfully earned his keep, watching over a yard that at the moment hosts three MG TDs, a Mini Cooper S, a Morris Minor station wagon, and a Triumph Herald. Dierker's private collection includes an Austin Cambridge and a Triumph Mayflower—"cars that if they're kept very nice, and very clean, in many years will still be worth absolutely nothing," Dierker notes.

And yet Ned guards everything as though it were a vintage Bentley. Among his more notable—*ahem*—collars was the interloper he treed on top of a Jaguar XJS. "Ned tried so hard to get at him, we had to repaint the entire car," says Dierker. More recently, a burglar trying to break in the back door turned to see Ned and his security team zeroing in. The perp ran *through* the chain-link gate, breaking it off its hinges.

For the most part, though, crack-enhanced entrepreneurs give Ned a wide berth in this city where he has achieved nearly mythic status—with a little help from his friends.

Ned enjoys considerable perks of canine celebrity. A local grocer brings him gallons of ice cream, the butcher shop brings along weekly allotments of raw meat and rib bones. The cops bring him chili dogs. The Goodwill thrift shop brings him couches, one of which he eats through every two months.

"From a veterinary standpoint," says Dr. Demanes, "his diet is pretty scary."

In the midst of a late-life voluptuousness worthy of Jake LaMotta—who also ate couches—Ned cannot last much longer. In fact, to get him to the vet's, Dierker now has to borrow Dr. Harvey's 1970 Citroën "safari" station wagon, because Ned can't jump into a truck, and no one's about to try to lift him. "I let the suspension on the Citroën bottom out and then put out a ramp for him to walk on."

Ned is one chili-dog away from eternity.

Bill Dierker will miss him. But Ned's protégé is waiting in the wings. A cross between a Rottweiler and a hydrophobic rat, this dog got his name when he attacked the otherwise harmless Thievin' Gene, who had come to the garage to sell a stolen battery. Gene, trying to run and still carry the battery, the

dog hanging off his pantleg, kept screaming, "Do he bite?!
Do he bite?! Do he bite?!"

So, naturally, Dierker named him Dewey.

from CAR AND DRIVER

Ebony, a Soldier

JOSEPH J. WHITE

I spent my first day with the 47th Scout Dog Platoon processing in and finding a place to bed down. In my free time, I wandered about the compound checking out the dogs and the training area with its wooden ramps and stacked barrels. The whole thing awed me, and I began to feel proud to be a part.

That night, I sat around with a couple of the other handlers and naturally the topic of finding a dog for me came up. Three dogs were without handlers, so the choice would not be complicated. I asked each of the guys which dog they would choose, and without hesitation they all responded the same— Ebony, she's the best there is. So, right then and there, Ebony and White became the newest team.

First thing the next morning, the training sergeant took me out to the kennels and introduced me to my new partner. I had never seen a black German Shepherd before, so I was stunned to see how beautiful she was and elated to see her happy and smiling. After all, most of the dogs were classically colored males and a bit on the aggressive side.

My trainer unhooked Ebony, commanded her to stay and told me to watch as he showed me how trained she was. She did all the basic commands off-leash, responding to both hand signals and verbal commands, which really impressed me. But it was her efforts on the obstacle course that sewed things up. You see, she not only conquered each challenge with ease, but she did so while expressing great joy. This dog loved to work, and it was truly beautiful to see her in action.

At the end of the demonstration, I was handed the leash and our work as a team began. Ebony had been a soldier since September 1967 and an active scout in Vietnam for more than a year, so she knew it all. I was the one who had to be trained. In reality, I should have been the one on the leash.

For almost an hour, I worked on the basic commands of heel, sit, stay, down, come, and I picked up on the program quickly. Then the instructor directed me to the obstacle course where Ebony worked as if we had been together for months. I felt great pride and honor. . . .

I was her CO, her leader and her master. And, although she knew what to do from the time we got on the supply bird, she also knew that she was to work at my command. The word that she was now waiting to hear was "search!" She would not start until she heard it. In fact, I had once forgotten to give her the command, and she literally blocked my path until I remembered. That dog taught me a great deal about being a good dog handler.

Most trails that lead away from mountain LZs dropped quickly, and this was no exception. As soon as we reached the nearby tree line, the trail began to pitch downward at such a steep angle it forced me to desperately grope for the smaller trees to keep from going head-over-heels. The battle continued for several yards at a time—a feat worthy of an athletic award considering the added weight of a full pack. Ebony, as usual, didn't seem to be having any extra difficulty at all. Instead, she was trotting up and down the trail with an ease that suggested she was part mountain goat.

The steepest part of the descent lasted for a full 15 minutes and didn't begin to level off until we were very near the bottom. All the clinking and clanging of equipment as the others fought their way down the incline eliminated any possibility for scouting. If the enemy was on the trail, we were certainly not going to surprise them. Normally, this would have increased my anxiety, but I was more concerned with the rivers of salty sweat flowing across my eyelids, down my nose and into my eye sockets. I wanted to wipe away the burning but my hands were occupied with maintaining balance—there wasn't a dry spot of clothing on me. The jungle humidity, combined with the intense strain of the descent, had forced open every pore in my body, from the top of my head down to the balls of my feet.

Finally, the trail bottomed out at roughly the point where it intersected the NVA route. Although I had known there was a major trail to work, the foreknowledge did little to discourage the fear. The feeling that I got was very much like someone driving through a strange city late at night, making a wrong turn, and ending up lost in the worst part of town. I would gladly have chosen to hack out a new trail away from that ribbon of terror, but being a dog handler prohibited that action. . . .

This path was used regularly by large numbers of unfriendly troops, and for us to follow it with our small force bordered on insanity. But, we had Ebony and felt confidence in her presence. A dog's reputation for giving an advantage was well documented by the saving of countless thousands of lives, and I was counting on that record to hold true now.

Ebony's nose was on hyper drive as she reacted to the smells the trail offered. She sniffed in one direction for a few feet then turned and sniffed in the other direction. All the while, her ears were panning the area for additional evidence of any obvious danger. But, there were no strange sounds and seeing her ears relax allowed me to do the same.

Once her initial sweeps were completed, Ebony returned to my immediate front in obvious anticipation of new instructions. I had known that the plan was for us to go left and follow the trail as it supposedly wound its way between the mountains. But, as super as the dog was, she could never know such things in advance. And even if she could, she would still choose to get the command directly from me.

I checked behind me to make sure that everyone was ready. Assured that they were, I again turned to catch Ebony's eye, gave her the simple signal of pointing to the left, and off she went. Her pace was like that of a prancing horse, but her attitude was like a top-notch detective. She knew what evidence needed to be discovered. The back and forth actions of her nose, eyes and ears were sure indications that she was hard at work.

We were only on the trail for five minutes when Ebony had her first alert of the mission. There was nothing visible, but it was quite obvious that she was hearing something strange.

I was level with the tops of my boots before we both realized that it was only an alert to something that belonged in the jungle. A family of gibbons appeared in the trees diving from branch to branch. Seeing the slender apes was refreshing, as it assured us all of the absence of danger.

I had seen gibbons many times before, but they were no less entertaining now. For several long minutes, I held my place and watched the show. I was both amazed and envious of their judgment and agility, and I was willing to wager that every zoo in the world would have loved to duplicate the scene. Each ape, both young and old, was diving from one tree top to the next, their bodies fully spread-eagled, literally flying above us. They seemed to be in constant motion, although their landings were causing the tree tops to bend to their absolute limits. At times, several apes would land together, totally defying those limits. . . .

We were again moving and able to hump along steadily for at least 20 uninterrupted minutes. Then we entered the area that Sergeant Rock had suggested as being a prime ambush spot. I immediately slowed our movement to nearly no movement at all. This particular section of the ravine was much wider than the rest, with vegetation as dense as we had seen— an ideal setting for a large enemy base. Split and drooping leaves from huge, wild banana trees hung over the largest ferns I could ever imagine, completely blocking out the sky. It was almost noon but there was little light getting through. It was a frightening situation, and my pace was reflective of my fear.

At some point, the trail began to curve and brighten. I was thankful for the additional light and the expanded visibility as it provided a much-needed boost to my courage. Every soldier likes the idea of cover, but, at the same time, needs to see all that can be seen. The fact that Ebony was black greatly increased my personal desire to see. When the jungle blacked out the sky, I often lost sight of her. If she was going to be my early warning, I had better see her signal. I was glad to see her at work again, but my joy was to be short-lived.

About midway into a rounded curve, Ebony suddenly became rigid with concentration—far more intense than with the apes. My eyes never left her as I threw my body quietly to the ground. There would be no stopping at the boot laces on this one. I knew she was onto something serious and had to get down level with the dirt in a hurry or risk being blown away. My K-9 buddy was detecting through sounds, the presence of the most dangerous of all animals—the two-legged kind.

The chain of men behind me followed my lead until all were down. Their actions must have looked like the choreographed peel of a seasoned flag corps, only much faster and not nearly as pretty.

I lay there in the damp coolness straining to see both Ebony and the unknown. I watched as she worked her ears against the unseen sound waves. One ear was fixed to the initial direction of hearing, while her nose and the other ear probed for additional clues. The muscles in her neck were tense and her coat glistened under the occasional ray of sun. Twenty-five seasoned soldiers lay behind me, hidden and fearful, while Ebony bravely scanned for an exact fix on what was threatening us.

Satisfied that she had the information available, she stealthily returned to my side. She hastened to give me a second warning. This time she stayed with me while again alerting to danger. Had I been directly behind her, I could have used her nose and ears like the sights on a rifle. But, this was not necessary because I had seen everything that I needed to know on her first alert.

Rock and another soldier quickly joined us. They, like everyone else, were eager to know the full status of our situation. The soldier with Rock was obviously nervous but the lieutenant was strangely calm. Perhaps he was simply hardened to such situations, or maybe it was because this was the exact spot where he had predicted trouble. In any event, his calmness was contagious, and I was grateful for it.

I shared my belief that Ebony had heard a substantial amount of movement and perhaps voices. It was not a single sniper or trail watcher, but rather a group of men. Perhaps there was a column or patrol similar to our own, or maybe a guard post protecting a base. These were my educated assumptions based solely on observation. I had watched as Ebony seemed to alert to several positions within one small area rather than one fixed place. This eliminated the idea of a sniper or trail watcher and strongly implied the presence of a multi-man position. She kept her attention focused on the area, which told me that the danger was staying put.

Reading the dog's alerts was never an exact science and a necessary part of a dog handler's job involved a lot of estimating and guessing. A handler only reports an alert as an absolute fact if he can clearly see the danger, which was rarely the case. Normally, the dog will alert well in advance of any sighting being possible. This enhanced the ability to stay alive, but it also added uncertainty to an analysis of the situation. Ebony had certainly heard some enemy presence, but I was only reporting my best guess as to what it might be. . . .

It took Rock just two minutes to decide exactly what needed to be done. He had spotted a small opening through the trees and had calculated that his best thumper man could fire a gas grenade through the opening into the suspected enemy position. Such an exploratory shot could produce a response, while never giving away our own position.

The third man with us returned to his position who was then replaced by the guy with the grenade launcher. This weapon was commonly called "the thumper" because of the thump-like sound it made when fired. Technically, it was the 40mm Grenade Launcher M79. It resembled a fat shotgun, was single shot, and broke open near the handle for loading. In the open, it could fire up to 400 yards. It could not produce rapid fire, but it was the ideal weapon for this particular situation.

Rock turned and made a few hand gestures telling the others to prepare for the worst, and to get ready to return fire if necessary. The gunner quietly slipped the gas round into its metal chamber and began to take aim. Rock whispered a brief final instruction to the man and the round was off.

The shot was absolutely perfect, landing exactly in the area of the alert. There was no explosion to confirm its purpose, but we could hear the crackling of escaping gas. With the lone exception of the gas-grenade sounds, it was strangely quiet. For some very long seconds all life seemed to be put on hold.

I looked to Ebony hoping to get a clue, but she, too, seemed to be on hold. As I looked away from her, I saw a change. She stiffened her ears and leaned forward a bit, and before I could question it I heard. Small limbs were being snapped and smaller bushes were being smashed. It sounded like a hunter had startled a buck in a thicket and the animal was in panicky retreat. That single sound of desperation was quickly joined by what seemed like a whole herd. And then it was over.

Some rays of sun made their way down to us turning the heavy air into a haze, blurring our vision as well as our minds. Rock asked me what I thought, and, although I was basically as lost as everyone else, I was able to report that the dog had relaxed considerably.

By the time the last of the gas was gone, we were ready to move. On Rock's word, we did just that. I gave Ebony her cue and she shot forward. I had to whistle her to a stop. She had no fear of what was ahead, but I did and worried that she might trip a mine or make some other fatal error.

As cautiously and quietly as was possible, we all pushed forward. My eyes were glued to the dog. No doubt about it, I was putting my very life on Ebony's ability to help keep me alive. In reality, there was very little choice in the matter as the surrounding jungle made seeing all but impossible. It was one of those special times when appreciation for the dog exceeds measurement and can only be described in terms of thankfulness.

I'm not sure how long it took us to reach a critical point in the trail because time seemed to have lost much of its meaning, but I shall never forget the feelings of fear that accompanied it. This particular place was critical, not only because it was very near to where the gas had landed but also because the trail became its own hazard. It was much wider than before, and it went straight as an arrow for a good 30 paces before making a radical turn to the left. Many of us could get all lined up in the open stretch and become dead meat in a hurry if anyone was waiting to catch us there. No sooner did we reach the straight part when Ebony again let her curiosity propel her faster than I wanted. I was so nervous that I did not chance making a sound to slow her.

Watching Ebony advance with such a child-like absence of fear pained me as if I were being forced to see her death. I slowed to a stop expecting to open fire in support of my four-legged buddy. I kept my eyes fixed on her until she reached the blind turn to the left. There she gave a very strong alert, and we all hit the ground. But, rather than staying fixed on the spot as she would with potential danger, she took a quick look back at me at the questioned area and again back to me. It was as though she wanted me to see something while strongly implying that all was okay. With this in mind, I got us going. Curiosity was moving my feet and I knew that could get me killed, but curiosity can be so powerful that it sometimes overcomes good sense.

I moved quickly down the straight section and cautiously peered around the blind corner. What I saw in the blind answered the entire mystery. It was the obvious source of Ebony's excitement and the shocking reality of what could have been. The brush was mashed down on both sides of the trail. A patrol of enemy soldiers had been unknowingly approaching us along the trail. They probably heard us first and formed an ambush at the blind. From the looks of things, it appeared that they could easily have killed many of us before we knew what had happened. Thanks be to God for Ebony because she turned the surprise around. And she single-handedly kept us all alive.

from EBONY AND WHITE

A Special Investigator

SHERRY BENNETT WARSHAUER

Onyx boarded the U.S. Air flight to Texas with Allegheny County Fire Marshal John Kaus and Police Investigator John Hudec of Tarentum, Pennsylvania. She wore the County Police Arson K-9 badge. She was expected; she had an assigned seat next to a widened floor space, as U.S. Air had arranged for her to be catered to. She would not be placed in the baggage compartment in a cage, as is required by the airline.

Onyx, a small black Labrador Retriever, had never been caged. Acknowledged as the best accelerant detection dog in the country, she was on her way to Waco, Texas. It was April of 1993. The entire country was looking for answers to the Waco catastrophe. Allegheny County Deputy Fire Marshal Thomas Hitchings, one of the fire investigators chosen by the federal government to conduct the independent investigation, indicated that the fire scene was a "dog" scene. He requested that the canine team he had worked with in the past be brought to the scene. This request was approved by Attorney General Janet Reno. Onyx was the only dog assigned to the investigating group and a key player in the investigation; she had been selected to work with the FBI, ATF and Texas Rangers.

The fire at the compound, which had been occupied by an armed religious cult known as the Branch Davidian, killed approximately eighty people and ended a fifty-one-day siege by federal agents. The 25,000-square-foot compound had been a raging inferno and was leveled to the ground in less than ten minutes. The investigation was needed to determine what caused the fire's rapid spread and to what extent it was aided by accelerants.

The investigators had to try to repress the obvious emotional impact of the sights and smells as they worked their way through a compound ridden with death and weaponry. Piles of munitions were so extensive that you could walk 10 to 20 feet without touching soil.

It was hot and windy. Temperatures rose into the 90s. It took Onyx about five minutes to tune out the general smell and focus on the stronger concentrations. Without Onyx's help, there would have been about 600 samples of debris that would have had to have been analyzed in a laboratory. She identified and alerted to about 100, therefore saving a great deal of time and money. Onyx worked for short periods and then rested in an air-conditioned van between sessions. Because of strong winds, electronic accelerant detectors would have been useless. This was a massive effort, with about 300 people working on the site at one time. The compound was divided into several areas, which were subdivided into 20-foot square sections. Onyx went through every section, while the arson team catalogued all of the evidence.

They spent seven days in Waco, with the team working twelve- to sixteen-hour days. The work was harrowing. At one point, Kaus and Onyx stepped over a live grenade that had not been detected in previous sweeps of the compound. It was found about fifteen minutes later by an FBI agent.

Infrared videotape, which had been taken during the fire

by an FBI aircraft, showed the fire starting in the same areas targeted by Onyx, confirming the accuracy of her detection.

There in the midst of the horror was Onyx, lightening the moment with her humor. When Hudec and Kaus went out to breakfast in Waco, they left Onyx in the hotel room with the television on, tuned to cartoons—her favorite. They did this so that she would not howl at people passing by. Hudec, with whom Onyx lives most of the time, said she is not permitted on the furniture in his home. However, she considers herself a guest in a hotel room. When they returned to the room, Onyx was lying under the covers, watching television.

The Connecticut State Police Canine Unit began training dogs in 1986 to detect petroleum distillate odors to help fire investigators determine accelerant use in fires of suspicious origins. . . .

Guide dogs in-training who exhibit too much energy and cannot be utilized as guiding eye dogs are often ideal candidates for sniffing out drugs, explosives or accelerants. The Connecticut State Police train dogs from all over the nation. Although several breeds are used in this field, Labrador Retrievers are most commonly used. Labs offer several advantages. As hunting dogs, they are very olfactory-oriented. Generally smaller than German Shepherd Dogs, Labs can maneuver more easily through the wreckage of a fire scene. Since Labs have shorter hair than Golden Retrievers or German Shepherd Dogs, they don't pick up as much debris on their coats from a fire scene.

Hudec and Kaus went to Connecticut in January of 1990 to look into an innovative program that paired dog and officer as an arson detection team, which proved to be considerably more effective than any existing technology. Kaus and Hudec fell in love with Onyx, who had been donated to the program by Guiding Eyes for the Blind. She was the friendliest and smallest of the dogs there, weighing in at only 55 pounds. They had come to Connecticut for information, but they were so impressed with the program and Onyx that they took her home. Onyx's training began in April of 1990. By October, Onyx and Hudec were ready.

In 1990, Onyx was the only arson dog in the state of Pennsylvania and one of only twenty such dogs in the world. She was the twelfth dog to graduate from the Connecticut State Police Academy. Onyx has been trained and is certified by the ATF to sniff out remnants of flammable substances used to start fires. Onyx was the second accelerant detection dog. The program started in 1989 with six dogs known in the world for this special ability.

Onyx started in the guide dog program, but was released. Her independent and inquisitive nature was put to good use in another field where she was destined to excel. She was trained to detect petroleum-based accelerants, such as gasoline, using the same reward method one would use to train a dog to sit, stay or obey other commands.

Labradors are known for their scenting ability. Their olfactory sense is said to be 97 percent accurate. An investigation can take three firefighters four to five hours, using state-of-the-art hydrocarbon odor-sensory devices. Some fifteen to twenty samples of potential accelerants are sent for laboratory analysis at a cost of $400.00 per sample. Many are not good, and locations of other accelerants may be overlooked. When a dog is brought in for an investigation, two to three samples are sent, and they know that they are good. They are confident that all the locations are found, and it usually takes a dog no more than twenty minutes to complete an investigation.

At a fire scene, Onyx will sit down and point when she recognizes a scent she is trained to detect. When Onyx smells accelerants, her brow and her ears go up, she wrinkles her forehead, she wags her tail and her entire body is at alert. In each case, she will receive a handful of kibbles as her reward for the find. If Onyx starts to salivate, they know that she is getting a scent and anticipating her reward. They are assured that it is an excellent hit. Samples are collected in metal containers, which are then removed to the outside. She alerts to them again to confirm the correct find. Each container is labeled with Onyx's very own sticker, the profile of a Labrador Retriever on a bright orange background with the words, "Onyx's Nose."

from EVERYDAY HEROES

Running Free

VICTORIA BREHM

I took him on as an act of charity. I'd just ended a relationship and was feeling the need to nurture something, and he certainly needed to be nurtured. "Take this dog," said the dog groomer, running her hand over his matted coat. "He needs a home. His owners don't want him, and he's miserable. He'll be on this table for at least 6 straight hours while I get the knots out of his fur."

Knowing how much an Afghan hound would demand in time and money, I took him anyway, giving in to an old impulsiveness that has gotten me into trouble more than once, and not only with dogs. He crawled, trembling, into the back of my car. When I got home and opened the car door, he bounded away.

As he ran into the wind, silver-gray coat floating, I thought if nothing else this dog named Zack is a truly beautiful creature. Half an hour later he was at the back door cringing, waiting to be punished for running free. When he realized he would be praised instead, he ate a huge dinner, inspected his new bed, flopped down and slept. He woke me at dawn by resting his chin on the mattress and licking my face.

I would soon discover that this time, at least, my impulsiveness would pay off: Zack was going to give me as much as I had given him. He would give me back a cherished but long-lost freedom.

The first time he accompanied me on my regular morning run in the park, the sight of him reduced two young girls to hysterics. Another day he helped the UPS man break the 4-minute mile. Shortly after that, the meter reader called me with terror in his voice because Zack had penned him in the closet with the gas meter. "That dog of yours," he gasped, "has got teeth like a wolf. Do you know that?"

I did not. The only part of his face I noticed was his nose poking into my face at 6:00 every morning. But I suddenly realized that if he scared that many people, if he really did look that fierce, I could run at night, something I hadn't done in years.

I am a small, middle-aged woman, and I live in a neighborhood that is long on hedges, trees and dark shadows. But running with Zack, I no longer have to be afraid of the shadows, because there is nothing in them that isn't going to be afraid of this dog. I finally know what it's like to be 6'2" with a voice like John Wayne and the bravado to match—nobody bothers you. The night is yours and you are free, and that is wonderful.

Now on warm spring nights I come home from teaching college classes, shed my professional clothes and drop the literature texts where they fall. I put on my sweats and Walkman. And Zack and I cruise through the dark streets to the beat of old rock and roll, simpler music from a simpler time.

Other runners, always men, avoid us. The shadows float past harmlessly. On the darkest streets, we run in the middle of the pavement and watch the stars. There are a lot of stars in Iowa City, something I'd never noticed before. The lights of the campus spread out like a small, glowing city seen from a plane. We are masters of all we survey: the lights, the dark streets, the stars. No one can threaten our dominion.

All over campus I see bulletins for the Iowa Women's Transit Society, which gives rides to women at night, and I am reminded of the danger in the shadows. The women in my classes carry whistles on their keychains; they ride the bus. If they are alone, they stay inside after dark. They would be foolish not to.

I, too, once stayed indoors at night. When Zack and I pick up the pace, I remember the bulletins. I think of the Central Park jogger. The radio plays "Lil' Red Riding Hood." I turn it up to get the beat, and my dog and I run on through the dark. Free.

from RUNNER'S WORLD

Arson Dog on Duty

TIM SIMMONS

---

*I*n the frigid predawn hours of Christmas 1993, a Phoenix, Ariz., man lay asleep in his bed. Dozing peacefully, he'd long put aside a dispute with a family acquaintance the evening before. But the acquaintance hadn't forgotten. Driven by the desire for revenge, the young man returned to the home and tossed a firebomb through the bedroom window, killing his victim and setting the home ablaze.

On a sweltering Phoenix evening some months later, a young woman argued with her ex-boyfriend. Hours later, the boyfriend returned to the second-story apartment with a friend and set the interior stairwell on fire with gasoline. With no other exit from the building, another second-floor resident was forced to drop her two children from a window before jumping herself. The children suffered minor injuries; the woman broke both legs. The intended victim, the girlfriend, was not at home at the time of the attack.

Who do these two arson cases have in common? Both were cracked by the Phoenix Fire Department's accelerant detection dog, Sharky, a 6-year-old black Labrador Retriever. With handler Capt. Mike Berggren, a department fire investigator,

Sharky found the sources of both fires, which a lab confirmed. His work led to a first-degree murder conviction in the first case and a felony conviction in the second.

The cases Sharky is involved in are not always so sordid.

Last summer, Berggren and Sharky responded to a house fire call. The fire had destroyed virtually everything the owners had. Both of their cats were missing, too. As the family's two children stood by on the verge of tears, Berggren pressed Sharky into service. Moments later, he found one cat hiding under a charred waterbed, the other under some clothing in a closet. Both were unharmed—though they didn't seem to appreciate the Lab sniffing and barking at them as much as the children did. At a fire station ceremony a few weeks later, the children presented Sharky with a huge bone as a reward.

In his four years as a member of the Phoenix Fire Department, Sharky has been involved in almost 200 arson investigations. None of those that reached court has ever been lost. He's been 100 percent effective, Berggren said.

He's considered one of the family and comes to work with Berggren almost every day. In his role as an accelerant detective dog, Sharky sniffs out trace amounts of ignitable liquids used to start fires. He spent two months training with the Maine State Police and six more weeks training with Berggren.

Sharky lives with him, sleeps wherever he likes and spends a lot of time in the back yard with Berggren's other dog, a male Great Dane named Duke.

His daily training regimen is based on a food reward system. Berggren is the only person allowed to feed Sharky. "He never eats without training," Berggren said. "To get fed, he has to identify or find something. Throughout the day, he receives all the food a dog his size requires." Sometimes Berggren puts droplets of an accelerant on various items such as wood, nylon or cotton, burns them, and Sharky has to identify which item had the droplets on it.

The fire department staff is accustomed to having Sharky in meetings. No bashful wallflower, Sharky makes his presence known. More than once, he has taken a firefighter down to the floor when playing.

But Sharky knows how to treat a lady. "I walked in one morning," said secretary Karen Warrington, "and he got up on his back two legs and gave me a kiss."

No sexual harassment charges were filed.

Accelerant detection dogs' careers can last five to seven years. What happens to Sharky then? "I think I get to keep him," Berggren said, grinning.

from DOG FANCY

The Dog
Nobody Wanted

COLLIN PERRY

S taring at the creature in the small cage at the shelter, Brian Gallagher—all six-foot-four, 254 pounds of him—knew he'd met his match. The dog's black eyes stared back fearlessly and challengingly.

"You don't want that one," an attendant said. "Nothin' but trouble."

"I'm a cop," Gallagher shot back. "Trouble's my business."

"Yeah, well, this dog ain't no turn-in from a little old lady. He was leading a pack that was running wild. Nobody wants him." The attendant motioned toward a door to the room where animals are put to sleep.

Gallagher looked at the card taped to the cage: *"Part German shepherd. Part husky. Think he's called King."* The dog growled, flashing gleaming white teeth. Greasy hair stood out around his neck, making his large head appear even bigger.

"A bit touchy are we, King?" Gallagher said. He took a towel from a paper bag, rolled it, and waved it slowly in front of the cage. King's eyes locked on like lasers. When Gallagher held it closer, the dog lunged, clamping his powerful jaws on the heavy wire mesh.

"Told you," said the attendant. "Too wild."

"Unlock it," Gallagher said.

"You kidding?"

"Go ahead. He'll be okay."

The attendant shook his head, unlocked the cage and quickly stepped back. Gallagher crouched, eye-level with King. The dog watched intently, growling deep in his throat.

"Atta boy," Gallagher said softly, slowly opening the cage. Carefully he held out his hand, palm down. The dog sniffed. Then the cop offered the rolled towel. At once, King snatched it. Seconds later, the towel lay in a shredded heap.

Gallagher moved back, allowing King out of the cage. The attendant flattened himself against the wall. "You *crazy*?"

King bounded out. His eyes passed over the frightened attendant and focused on Gallagher, who threw another rolled towel down the 60-foot hall. King was off like a rocket. Halfway down, he started skidding on the polished floor. His backside crashed against the far wall. But he had the towel, which he raced back to Gallagher.

He's got real spirit, thought Gallagher as the two played tug of war. Then he tried to pull King back into his cage by tugging the towel. Instantly, King's massive jaws clamped around his forearm.

"Okay, you win," Gallagher said in a conciliatory tone. "You don't like being told what to do. Neither do I." Slowly he reached for the towel with his free hand and tossed it into the cage. As if to say, "Don't try that again!" King applied a bit more pressure before releasing Gallagher's arm. Then, on his own, he trotted into his cage.

"Put a hold on that dog," Gallagher told the wide-eyed attendant. "I'll be back to pick him up."

As Brian Gallagher left the shelter on Manhattan's Upper East Side that blustery March day in 1989, he was already having second thoughts. *It's nuts. How do I know that dog won't tear me apart—like the towels?*

He remembered his former canine partner—a magnificent white German shepherd named Buddy. For seven years, Gallagher and Buddy had been inseparable, patrolling by day for Metro-North Railroad and going home together at night. Then the unthinkable happened. Working and living with Buddy, Gallagher began experiencing serious allergic reactions. He got dizzy and short of breath. He had severe coughing fits, and his face would swell until his eyes were puffy slits. In that condition, he knew he might become a danger to others.

Tearfully, Gallagher placed Buddy in a foster home. Within months the dog was dead.

Gallagher joined the New York City Police Department and not long after faced near-death as he dragged an accident victim from an exploding car. Two days later, a robbery suspect aimed a shotgun at Gallagher's head. Time stood still as Gallagher awaited the blast. He heard a *click*—but the gun misfired.

That's when Gallagher began thinking of quitting the force. "I just can't hack it anymore," he told a chief.

"What about working with dogs again?" asked the chief.

"My wife can't take the dog hair," he lied. Gallagher had never told his boss at Metro-North why he'd left the canine division.

"So what about narcotics? Those dogs don't go home with you. You take them out in eight-hour shifts, and they're back in the kennel. Keeps their sense of smell sharper."

"That so?" It might be worth the risk—if he could find the right dog.

Now as he listened to the March wind, he thought, *Okay, I may be nuts—but I think that wild dog in there would be a super cop.*

Gallagher immediately began King's training at the police department's Canine Center in Brooklyn. There, a 5-by-30-foot training wall held a number of "traps"—small pockets covered with cardboard. In one, Gallagher had placed King's "toy"—a rolled-up towel—only now it was laced with heroin. Could he find it by scent?

King seemed uninterested as Gallagher led him to the wall on his choke leash. Then the dog heard a rustle from a nearby bush and began straining toward it, barking furiously. The other kennel dogs joined in.

"Easy, King, easy," yelled Gallagher above the din.

"Can't you keep that mutt quiet, Gallagher?" Another officer had appeared in the doorway of the nearby office trailer. Then he paused, curious. "How's he doing?"

"First rate," Gallagher said confidently. Then he muttered under his breath to King, "C'mon, don't make a jackass out of me! Find the towel!" Instead, King pulled Gallagher toward the far end of the wall and started scratching on an empty trap.

"First rate, all right." The other officer laughed.

"Gotta be some traces of drugs in there," explained Gallagher, only half believing it himself. When the officer left, Gallagher said, "Okay, King, let's take a walk, then call it a day."

Walking with King through the streets of Brooklyn, Gallagher recalled his own training and how the instructor had told the students to talk constantly to their canine recruits to build trust.

"But what do we *say* to a dog?" one student had asked.

"Tell him your life story," the instructor had replied. And that's exactly what Gallagher did now. "Buddy was bigger than you, King—and, let's face it, pal, a lot prettier," he confided. "But you've got the edge in toughness."

Then the man knelt and held the dog's huge head in both hands. "Listen up, friend. I already lost one dog, and I'm not about to lose another. I have faith in you. You've got to stop playing around!"

"New dog?" The narcotics detective was standing outside a tenement, waiting to go in for a search.

"Yeah," replied Gallagher nervously. "Name's King."

The dog looked scruffier than ever. He'd smashed his left ear, which now swiveled sideways while the other stood straight as a spike. With his tongue dangling out, he looked slightly deranged.

The detective seemed skeptical. "We've been looking for two hours and can't find a thing. So whenever you and King there are ready . . . "

Two weeks before, King had passed his final test, but barely. He'd found the drugs the trainers had planted, but he had also gleefully torn an old mattress to shreds. Now came his first real job. *If he tears up a couch and there's nothing there, we're dead,* thought Gallagher as the dog raced up the tenement stairs, pulling him along.

With King bounding ahead, Gallagher entered the apartment. Two young suspects sat casually at the kitchen table, eating pizza. "Hey, keep that dog under control," one of them said.

King searched the living room, then the bedroom. Back in the kitchen, he began to growl and whine. As the men at the table watched intently, he went to the oven, where the pizza was, and scratched on the door. "Pizza dog," snickered one of the men.

Embarrassed, Gallagher directed King to the cupboards and

the refrigerator. But King still strained toward the oven door.

"I guess that wraps it," sighed the detective. "You guys lucked out this time. Gallagher, thanks for your help."

Gallagher, mortified, started dragging King across the linoleum floor. Then he stopped. *King hates pizza,* he thought. Opening the oven door, he flipped up the pizza box lid.

"We checked that," the detective said.

King pawed the door again, and Gallagher understood in a flash. He directed the detective to unscrew the oven door. As he did, one of the suspects bolted. Instantly King leapt and, using his big head like a battering ram, knocked the man down. Then he stood over him, growling.

The detective pried the door apart. Tucked neatly behind the insulation were bags of white powder. The detective looked at the stash, then at King, then at the two men. "Parmesan, anyone?"

In practically no time King had established a reputation for an uncanny nose. He traveled to airports, seaports and houses. Telltale drug traces pointed the dog to fake panels, hidden trap doors, plastic bags sealed within plastic bags. Over the next few years, King uncovered thousands of kilos of illicit narcotics. But his greatest challenge was to come on January 23, 1994.

It was an ordinary-looking utility truck, with storage boxes built in under the short, flat bed. Alert cops took its driver and a friend—suspected drug dealers—into custody. The truck was impounded.

"I know this thing is hot," said the detective in charge, slapping the bed of the truck. "But we can't hold these guys forever. Better get King over here."

Half an hour later, a dark-blue van pulled into the precinct.

Gallagher climbed out and opened the back. King was already barking excitedly and thrashing his tail.

"King, old buddy! How ya doin'!" the cops greeted him. The dog jumped out to receive affectionate pats on the head.

Then he walked slowly around the suspect truck and sniffed. Approaching the rear, he stopped abruptly, stood on his hind legs, did a little dance and whined.

"It's gotta be somewhere in the truck bed," Gallagher said.

A warrant was issued, and the laborious work of sawing through the bed began. As the Queens district attorney paced, the men cut through the first layer of metal. Nothing.

The DA frowned. "Are you guys sure there's something here?"

"Don't know," said the detective, looking more tense. "Gallagher?"

Gallagher shrugged. "If King says it's there, it's there."

After they cut through more layers of steel, a hidden trap was finally revealed. Inside, running the entire length of the truck's bed, were bag after bag of cocaine. They totaled 182 kilos and had a street value of $20 million—one of the largest narcotics seizures in New York history.

Gallagher stroked King's massive head, pushing his swivel ear back. "You did good, ya crazy mutt. No more work today. Now," he said, holding a rolled-up towel, "we play!"

"NYPD Dog Hits The Big One!" read the headline in *Canine Courier,* the journal of the United States Police Canine Association. Today King continues his career with a reputation as the No. 1 "narco" dog in New York City—all, as the *Courier* noted, "from the dog nobody wanted."

Brian Gallagher still hunts with King every day—only now a gold detective badge is pinned to Gallagher's shirt. He conducts training seminars across the country and teaches at the John Jay College of Criminal Justice.

When student cops ask him how to train a dog to become like King, Gallagher says, "You can mold most any dog into a good canine cop. But King? He's molded *my* life. He's truly a once-in-a-lifetime dog."

from READER'S DIGEST

IN THE SPOTLIGHT

"There is a time for everything, and a season for every activity under heaven."

ECCLESIASTES 3:1

$\mathcal{A}$nyone with an animal in the family knows they love to perform. Just throw a toy in the air and you'll be treated to an acrobatic spectacular. But there are some animals who perform far beyond our expectations, and many have had successful careers. Some compete for awards and some delight us as actors. Curiously, most of them didn't start out to be celebrities. In fact, some were considered losers—until somebody spotted their exceptional qualities and took the time to develop them. So you could say that, behind every celebrity animal, there's a person who truly appreciates him.

My Hero

VAN VARNER

When I was a skinny eighteen-year-old fresh in the service during World War II, I made an impetuous trip to see a boyhood hero of mine. With a precious pass in my uniform pocket, I thumbed my way on empty Georgia roads, sat up all night on an unheated Southern Railway coach, but finally pulled into Lexington, Kentucky. At the USO, a motherly-looking volunteer was just opening up. "Please, ma'am," I said, "can you tell me how I can find Man O'War?"

Would you believe that nice woman couldn't believe I'd made the long trip just to see him? Only the greatest thoroughbred that ever lived, that's all! He was old, twenty-seven, and I had to see him before either he or I died. That's the way we were in wartime.

Well, there were all kinds of phone calls with talk about gas coupons, but soon I was being driven out to Faraway Farm where an elderly man, Will Harbut, was actually waiting for me. Will was Man O'War's friend and groom—they were never apart. In a large green-painted shed, we crossed to a stall where Will rolled back the door.

"Okay, soldier boy, here he is, 'Big Red,' de mostest hoss."

I stared, mouth open.

Will talked at length about "Red's" speed, his stamina, his

courage. I stared at the hero I'd come so far to see. And heroic he was, a massive animal with a coat of polished copper, a head held high, eyes looking beyond me with an imperial gaze. And ancient he was (a human would have been in his nineties) but the fire was still there.

"Come on," Will said, "it's okay," and I reached out and placed my hand on the head of Man O'War.

It's a good thing to have heroes. Seeing that great thorough-bred gave my life romance, ardor. It even deepened my faith in the Almighty, for no one could look at Man O'War without knowing that only God could create an animal so powerful, and yet so noble.

Lassie—a.k.a. Pal

TIM JONES

The short story "Lassie Come Home" first appeared in the December 17, 1938, issue of the *Saturday Evening Post*. It told of a Scottish boy separated from his faithful collie and of the dog's thousand-mile journey across the rough Scottish landscape to rejoin his master. Readers responded so strongly to the story that author Eric Knight expanded it into a novel, which was published in 1940. By 1943, the story reached Hollywood, where a lack of scripts and, for that matter, movie stars prompted the Metro Goldwyn Mayer studio to begin production of a motion picture version.

To make the movie *Lassie Come Home*, the studio needed a star—not just a companion for a human actor, but a dog who could carry the lead role. Movie-makers had avoided collies in the past, finding them too temperamental for the long hours around the bustling movie sets. This role demanded a collie, though, so director Fred Wilcox began his search for the perfect Lassie.

At his brand-new kennel in North Hollywood, trainer Rudd Weatherwax read an advertisement calling for a movie collie. He thought he had just the dog. In business for just a few weeks, Weatherwax had been hired to work with a collie named Pal, to train away some of his many bad habits. The dog chased motorcycles, barked constantly, chewed every-thing he could get his teeth around, and wasn't even house-broken. Though he was a full-blooded collie, Pal didn't meet show criteria. His eyes were too large, his head too broad, and his hair too dark for the minions of the dog show circuit. Weatherwax quickly recognized that, despite his drawbacks, Pal possessed tremendous intelligence. As the owner was happy to be rid of the poorly behaved collie, Weatherwax bought Pal for ten dollars and took him through six months of intensive training.

When the call came for a Lassie, Pal had been sent to a friend's ranch, where he had the freedom to roam until there was room for him again at the North Hollywood kennel. Weatherwax came to retrieve Pal and take him to the tryout. But when Weatherwax called for Pal, the dog that came run-ning didn't have the fine coat with the full ruff that Weatherwax had remembered. Instead, the dog's coat was a mess, all full of burrs, with patches of fur ripped out. Pal looked more like a pound dog than a movie star.

Weatherwax did what he could with Pal's coat and took the mangy-looking dog to the designated field for the tryout, where 300 other collies were also waiting. The movie produc-ers didn't even give Pal a first glance. They walked right by without a nod. Still, they didn't find their perfect dog, either. When that tryout failed, Wilcox began a nationwide search. He settled on a beautiful show collie sometime later, but found that dog to be dumb and skittish. When the cameras started whirring, the show dog ran away and hid from the noise.

Weatherwax learned the movie crew still was looking for the perfect collie. By that time, Pal's coat had grown full again under his trainer's constant brushing and trimming. Weatherwax telephoned Wilcox to say he had "another dog" that would be perfect for the part. He was invited to a meeting and at this one, the carefully groomed Pal trotted up to Wilcox, sat on his haunches, and lifted his right paw to shake hands. Impressed, the director asked Weatherwax to put Pal through his paces. Once Pal had performed a series of exercises, mostly to silent hand commands, Wilcox called for a screen test. The physical deficiencies that had denied Pal show status proved to be attributes for a film star. His dark hair photographed well, and his large head projected the intelligence expected of Lassie's character. It was his eyes, though, those eyes too large for show judges, that emoted on the screen and gave him a personality that reached out to the audience. One day after his screen test, the studio signed Pal to a contract.

Pal's biggest test was yet to come. For the first scene filmed for *Lassie Come Home,* Pal had to swim the San Joaquin River, simulating Lassie's crossing of the Tweed River between Scotland and England. Weatherwax rowed Pal to the center of the river. At the indication from the director and a command from his trainer, Pal jumped from the boat into the river. He swam past another boat, containing a film crew, and headed right to a camera on shore. According to Weatherwax, Pal responded perfectly to his hand signals. When he reached shore, Pal climbed from the water, his tail between his legs and his head down, as if he were exhausted. He slinked to a point in front of the camera, laid down, and closed his eyes. The performance made even his trainer choke up. Wilcox commented to Weatherwax, "Pal jumped into that water, and Lassie climbed out."

Lassie Come Home opened to almost universally rave reviews. The *New York Times* reported that the movie provided "at least a partial solution to the present dearth of Hollywood leading men."

As Lassie, Pal made five more movies, starring with some of Hollywood's biggest stars, including Elizabeth Taylor. . . .

Lassie also had a radio show in which Pal barked, whined, and yelped on command to complement the voices of the human characters. In 1953 Lassie went to television in what would become one of the longest-running adventure shows ever. At least two generations of American children grew up with Lassie's pals—first Jeff, then Timmy—and watched her later adventures with the U.S. Forest Service. The show, starring seven generations of Lassies, ran for eighteen years and still appears in syndicated reruns.

Pal, the original Lassie, died at the age of nineteen, probably the richest and surely the most successful of all dog movie stars.

from DOG HEROES

Jack—the Horse That Had to Be Ours

CATHY GLADWIN

When Jack came into our lives it was almost like an answer to prayer. And yet I couldn't know then that this handsome bay thoroughbred was an answer in more ways than one.

The odd thing was that, even though my husband, Doug, had no horse to ride, at Christmas I gave him a pair of chaps and a black velvet riding hat. Doug loved horses, but it had been a dozen years since he'd ridden regularly.

We'd been scrimping and saving for a long time, with me working as a floral designer while Doug went to graduate school. Our marriage of eight years was a good one, though there were times when I couldn't help feeling a kind of empti-ness, which I figured was because we were unable to have children. Well, anyway, now that we had our own home here in Fort Collins and Doug was pretty well established as a wildlife biologist, I thought the time had come when Doug should be back with horses again.

Nearby we found an English training stable called Four Winds. It was like the one Doug had worked at as a boy back east when he had mucked out stalls, had groomed horses and had even shown them. Riding in open jumper classes, he had won several show-jumping championships. And there was one mount in particular that Doug loved and had won a handful of blue ribbons on, a quarter horse named Jack.

Now Doug put on the chaps and hat and started riding and jumping again. I could feel his happiness. Then one day in May Doug came home from Four Winds, all flushed and excited. Words tumbled out of him. "Cathy, I've found a horse. One of the trainers had me ride him. He's a beaut. I know I could turn him into a jumper. He's frisky and fast and he's for sale!"

And strangely enough, his name was Jack.

We drove out to the stable and Doug led Jack out of his stall into the walking ring. At first I didn't see what Doug saw. This eight-year-old former racehorse was frisky all right, almost too frisky, snorting and pawing the ground, and he was grossly underweight. No wonder his owners wanted to sell him.

Then Doug slipped into the saddle and took a firm hold of the reins. Jack tossed his head, his black mane flying, and then quieted at Doug's touch. Tall, willowy Doug leaned forward in the saddle. As Jack began to move about the ring, horse and man in perfect synchronization, I knew that these two belonged together.

Even when we asked our veterinarian to check him out, the doctor took one look at us and said, "It looks like you've made your minds up already."

We had.

But Jack was a challenge. He had raw talent that would require all of Doug's skill as a trainer to bring out if he were to be turned into a successful jumper. The first thing we did when we owned him was double his feed, from two flakes of hay a day to four, from two pounds of sweet grain to four. Gradually he began to fill out.

My job was to groom Jack, and even though I loved to curry him and make his reddish-brown coat shine, Jack was still nervous and skittish with me. One evening as I was scraping the mud off his hooves, I threw a white towel on his back. Out of the corner of his eye, Jack saw it and bolted in fear, breaking clear through the chain on his halter. Another time when I was walking him, he lifted my small frame off the ground with his reins. But I grew fond of even his skittishness, as a mother loves her children no less for any of their faults.

Doug progressed in his training. He had more time to work with Jack when we moved him to a stable close to home. Soon Doug was schooling Jack over fences, and little by little the fences got higher—up to six feet. Jack had a long stride, falling in a graceful arc as he jumped.

Soon we knew we had a winner, a jumper we could show, a horse that was the envy of the stable. A local horseman even offered to buy Jack. "I wouldn't take any money for him," Doug proudly said.

In December we were at the stable one day after Doug had come back from a long energetic ride on Jack. We had put him in his stall, but two weeks earlier he had broken the door that separated it from his smaller, outer pen. That December day we were in a nearby field, trying to find a goose someone had shot. Suddenly a stablegirl came running.

"Jack is trying to roll in the little pen," she said. We took off running. That pen was too small for him. If he lay down in it, he could easily feel trapped and become frightened.

We rushed to his pen, but it was too late. By the time we got there he was lying on his back wedged up against the barn wall, cast. He flailed aimlessly, trying to get up. There was a look of helpless panic in his eyes. His hooves pounded against the wall. Before we could do anything, he kicked his rear left hoof through the sheet-metal wall.

"Oh, no!" I cried. The sharp edge of the metal pierced his lower leg. Blood spurted everywhere.

"Cathy, go home," Doug shouted.

I was horrified. I couldn't move. I watched, stunned, as Doug got him up and, with Jack hobbling on three legs, pulled him to the trailer.

"Cathy, go home," Doug said again.

The trailer door closed. Blood was dripping out the back. I knew they were going to the Colorado State University Veterinary Teaching Hospital, about five minutes away. I knew I had to follow them, but I was afraid, afraid for my husband as much as for our horse.

The veterinarian at the hospital brought up the possibility of putting Jack down.

"No." Doug was adamant. The man who had waited all his life to own his own horse wasn't going to give up yet.

The doctor stopped the bleeding from the severed artery. We waited in a daze while the wound was cleaned and a plaster cast was put on Jack to protect the wound. "Even if he survives," he warned Doug, "there'll be no jumping for *this* horse."

Five hours later I saw Jack, still lathered in sweat. He was standing but scared, on medication, not showing any awareness of who we were.

I drove home. Doug said he'd walk. It was a moment of crisis, and yet we couldn't face it together. I sat behind the wheel when I got home, crying. I felt helpless. I had an urge to do something I hadn't done for years. I wanted to pray.

I'd grown up with the church. Once I'd loved to sing in the choir and say the Psalms. But ever since our marriage, I'd wandered away. Doug wouldn't come to worship with me; a nature person, he felt praising God in the open air on a mountain hike was enough. He said he didn't need to belong to a community of believers to believe. I didn't like to go to church alone, so I didn't go. And I thought less and less about God.

Now, feeling very much alone, I turned to Him.

Our house was silent for the next few days. Doug went into a depression that I'd never seen before. Jack was now a part of him, and he couldn't cope with the possibility of losing him. He would sit in his chair staring into space. He would lie disconsolately on the couch worrying about Jack. All I could do was pray.

Our visits to the hospital were disheartening. Jack would gaze at us uncomprehendingly. He didn't even know who we were. Thrashing about, he broke his cast, and a new one had to be made. When we talked to the doctors, they only shook their heads. They held out little hope for his improvement.

Then one Sunday morning two weeks after the accident, I woke up to find Doug gone. There was no note, no message telling me where he was or when he'd come home.

Around noon he returned, wearing a coat and tie.

"Where have you been?" I asked, trying to hide my anxiety.

He smiled sheepishly. He draped his necktie on the back of a kitchen chair. "To church," he replied.

I almost dropped my coffee mug. "Where?"

"The corner." There was an octagonal brick church, Foothills Assembly of God, about four blocks from us. We'd driven by it hundreds of times.

"Cathy, I want that horse to live," Doug continued. "I didn't know where else to turn. All I could do was pray. So yesterday I went to that church to pray. I met the pastor and told him I was losing Jack. He welcomed me and helped me.

"Then today when I went back—at first I stood in the last row. Then Pastor Taylor saw me and said from the pulpit, 'There's my friend Doug. Come on up and have a seat, Doug.' I did."

That was the first Sunday. The next Sunday we both went to church, and the next and the next. The people were friendly, coming up and introducing themselves. We talked about Jack to those who seemed interested. They didn't think it odd that we were praying for a horse. "We'll keep him in our prayers too," they said.

Sunday after Sunday I saw that we weren't alone. Pastor Taylor with his reassuring manner and Texas drawl always offered a comforting word, and the congregation gave us continual support. Strangely enough, as Doug and I grew stronger spiritually, Jack grew stronger physically. It was as though God was working on all of us at once. As Jack began his therapy, walking first only 50 yards, then 100, then 200, similarly we were taking steps that were bringing us to a fuller faith.

A week before Jack was released from the hospital, Doug and I went forward at an altar call, asking Jesus into our lives, and we gave God everything: hopes, our dreams, ourselves, even our horse.

Not long after that, on an April afternoon, Doug picked me up at work. He was wearing his riding boots and he had a peculiar grin on his face. We were stopped in traffic behind a Ford Bronco. On the spare tire in the back was a picture of a bucking bronco.

"You see that horse?" Doug said. "That's Jack."

"What?"

"I took him to the ring and turned him out. He ran and jumped. He's just like that bronco on the tire."

I had to go to the stable to see for myself. There was Jack, tossing his black mane with his head held high. His fire had returned. When I walked him, he tried to canter in place. It would be months before he was running and jumping, gobbling up the ground with his usual long strides and leaping over fences, but he was a horse again.

I thanked God for the way He'd worked in our lives. We'd been looking for something, something to fill that emptiness I'd worried about. It was as though we'd come home to God on horseback.

Be Careful—You Might Let Out a Bear

GARY RICHMOND

I'll never forget the feelings I experienced when two shiny new keys were pressed firmly into my trembling hands. They weren't just any keys. These keys gave me access to all the cages at the Los Angeles Zoo. The supervisor admonished me solemnly concerning the use and care of these keys.

"Richmond," he said, "these keys will let you in to care for millions of dollars worth of animals. Some of them could never be replaced, but you could be, if you catch my drift. Some of the animals would hurt themselves if they got out, and more significantly, they might hurt and even kill somebody. You wouldn't want that on your conscience.

"And, Richmond, don't lose the keys. The big boys in administration don't take it too well if you lose the keys. It works out best if they don't hear your name much until you pass probation six months from now."

The longer we talked, the heavier the keys became. I discovered that most of the veterans (five years or more of service) had let out animals. And if I stayed at the zoo, sooner or later that would happen to me. Somehow my job security was tied to how I cared for these keys, and they seemed heavier still.

The supervisor gave me several tips on key care, use, and safety, and emphasized the value of getting into a routine. "Consistency is your best safeguard," he said. "Do your routine the same way at every exhibit. Develop a good habit and don't vary your routine."

I took him seriously and performed flawlessly for four months. I received sterling evaluations for my safety habits—but then one day I made a mistake.

I wouldn't be able to tell you why my routine varied, but somehow it did, and with the most dangerous animal at the zoo. Ivan was a polar bear who weighed well over 900 pounds and had killed two prospective mates. He hated people and never missed an opportunity to attempt to grab them as they passed by his cage. Many of us had experienced nightmares featuring Ivan. And one of the concerns most discussed among the keepers was the horrifying question, "What if Ivan got out?"

For more than 100 consecutive workdays I had cared for this nightmare, never coming close to making a mistake. Then one day I let him out of his night quarters into the sparkling morning sunshine by pulling a lever that lifted a 500-pound steel guillotine door. No sooner had he passed under it than I realized that the steel door that had given me access to the outside exhibit (where Ivan was now) was still wide open. At any minute he might be walking down the hall and around the corner. My inclination was to run. Not wanting to be fired, however, I chose to stay.

I lifted the guillotine door again, and to my relief, Ivan was in view. He was a creature of routine, and he always spent the first hour of his morning pacing. His pattern was L-shaped. He would walk from the door five steps straight out and then turn right for three steps. He would then rock back and forth and come back to the guillotine door, which he would bump with his head. He would repeat that cycle for one hour and then rest.

I timed Ivan's pacing cycle and determined that I had 17 seconds to run down the hallway and shut the open door. I staked my life on his consistency. He didn't seem to notice the wide-open door, which was unusual. Animals tend to notice any changes in their environment.

I decided that when Ivan made his next turn, I would run down the L-shaped concrete hallway, hoping upon hope that I would not see Ivan.

When he turned, I ran. With every step my knees weakened. My heart pounded so hard I felt sure it would burst from fear. I made the corner and faced the critical moment. Ivan was still out of sight; I lunged for the door handle. As I reached for the handle I looked to the right. There was the bear, eight feet away. Our eyes met. His were cold and unfeeling and I'm sure mine expressed all the terror that filled the moment. I pulled the huge steel door with all my strength. It clanged shut and the clasp was secured. My knees buckled and I fell to the floor racked by the effect of too much adrenaline. I looked up, and Ivan was staring at me through the viewing window of the hallway door.

I had almost let out a bear—the worst bear at the zoo. All because I did not adhere to a simple habit I had followed to keep animals from escaping their cages.

from IT'S A JUNGLE OUT THERE

Gilmore and Roscoe

K. C. TESSENDORF

Early in 1930, a male lion cub was born near Hollywood, California. The breeder saw the cub as a fine specimen and looked hopefully toward the movie studios. Little did he know that this lion, who would be named Gilmore, would grow up in the sky! Roscoe Turner would be the means. Out of Corinth, Mississippi, Turner adorned the skies during the aerial stunt show heyday of the 1920s, as both a skilled pilot and flying's greatest publicity hound.

In those days, typical stunt pilots toured Middle America in soiled, smelly mechanic's garb. Most of them had gruff dispositions and were quite clannish—they talked to other airmen about airplanes. Not so Roscoe Turner. This handsome six-footer sported a waxed moustache, dressing elegantly. A typical "uniform" of Turner's design included a sky-blue jacket covered with diamond-spangled wings, white shirt and black tie, riding breeches, swell leather boots and a two-tone, goggled helmet.

Though jeered by rival pilots, Turner's panache drew reporters to the ever-welcoming flier and produced the newspaper stories that promoted his career. At the end of the 1920s a new corporate fad appeared, especially among oil companies. The companies would buy swift, showy airplanes and

197

hire popular pilots as flying advertisements. Roscoe Turner talked himself into flying for California's Gilmore Oil Company. A lion-head was the company's logo, so it wasn't long before the inspiration of "a flying lion!" came to Turner who chose Gilmore when he went looking for his flying lion. Though the asking price was beyond his means, the slick, honey-tongued pilot convinced the breeder that the high-flying team would put the lion farm in the spotlight and make it famous. Roscoe Turner received the 17-pound Gilmore for free.

Turner, so personable with humans, quickly bonded with baby Gilmore, whose waking hours soon became boring without Turner in sight. The pilot hadn't gotten the little lion to hide him. Almost everywhere Turner went, Gilmore came along on a leash, with the lion mimicking the flier's friendly social moves. Gilmore let strangers pet him, and he didn't bristle at cats or dogs. Even Turner's pet dog played cautiously with Gilmore.

After he was housebroken, Gilmore was considered ready for aerial duty. On the first flight, and on many thereafter, Turner's wife, Carline, went along in the small cabin. Turner would be barely in sight, behind and above her in the open cockpit, flying the Lockheed aircraft named *Gilmore Lion.* As the maiden voyage became airborne, Gilmore took a flying leap into Carline's lap and stayed there! . . .

When Gilmore had mastered air travel, "the flying lion" made every airport visit memorable. Typically, on parking the plane at the terminal, Turner would release Gilmore. Gilmore, in a friendly fashion, would lope forward to join the crowd . . . what crowd? A lot of people got a lot of exercise escaping the little lion's imagined jaws of death! These antics gave the press still more opportunities to feature Gilmore, Turner and the oil company.

Roscoe Turner once again saw opportunity when a humane society publicly asked what would happen to the lion if there was an airborne emergency. Fliers had parachutes, but what about lions? The short answer was that the devoted pair would jump as a unit beneath Turner's parachute. But Roscoe Turner made a big fuss of crafting a special small (and later a larger) parachute for Gilmore. The ripcord's end was tied to the plane so that the falling lion's parachute would surely be jerked open. Turner also fashioned Gilmore's own oxygen mask—and saw to it that the press was there.

In the 1930s, air racing—racing around a pylon-marked course—and long-distance record setting were both very popular. An ambitious pilot could gain glory by racing. Turner, already an experienced air racer, decided to go after the coast-to-coast speed record then held by Charles Lindbergh. And when the *Gilmore Lion* roared out of Los Angeles, its airworthy namesake was aboard.

It was not a well-disposed journey; weather demons lurked across America. Above New Mexico, headwinds and turbulence buffeted the aircraft. Worried Gilmore, now grown to adolescence, squirmed up into the cockpit with Turner—an awkward fit! The pilot seriously considered abandoning the trembling plane. But then Turner thought about Gilmore floating down into cattle country; would somebody shoot him on sight?

Turner shoved Gilmore back into the cabin and flew the sturdy Lockheed through the churning atmosphere into Wichita, Kansas, for quick refueling and horsemeat for Gilmore, and then continued east, where a final battle with headwinds forced them to land, out of fuel, a little short of New York City.

Nevertheless, two weeks later, the pair's return flight was a triumph! The new east-west record of 18 hours, 42 minutes must have been a trial to ever-patient Gilmore. He earned his lion's share! The homesick lion squashed Carline's lap all the way home from the airport.

With Gilmore grown obedient to Turner's commands and willing to follow at his heels, the lion was often free of the leash. If Roscoe Turner went to a business appointment, Gilmore went too, and sat solemnly listening to the chatter of the salesmen. In restaurants Gilmore did not beg for food, though lying under the table he might chew lightly on a patron's shoes. Gilmore always shared Turner's hotel rooms. The elegant pilot joked that it kept the ladies away.

The adolescent Gilmore did make a few goofs. Like the time a gentleman that Turner was trying mightily to impress was driving his limousine, Turner beside him and Gilmore in the back seat. When they halted at a red light, Gilmore impulsively licked the driver's neck. It felt like a hot rasp! The gentleman's foot jolted the accelerator and the great car leaped screeching into the flow of traffic!

Gilmore was overwhelmed by the scent of horsemeat on the hoof. Twice he caused great commotion, though he didn't injure the animals. The second time, the victim bore a mounted policeman. The horse bolted to escape Gilmore's attention, unseating the policeman as he did so. Roscoe Turner and Gilmore escaped the law by way of a hotel freight elevator.

Around the time Gilmore grew to 150 pounds, his flying days dimmed. But Turner continued to display Gilmore at the airport. When the flier arrived home in his plane, his big friend embraced Turner amid the pop of flashbulbs and the whirr of movie cameras. As the years passed, the pair saw less of each other. Then Roscoe Turner moved to Indianapolis to start up a new airline. Gilmore remained in California, comfortably set up at Turner's expense, at his original owner's lion farm.

During the war in the 1940s, several years passed between meetings of the old partners. On one occasion in 1946, Turner was super-confident, telling the manager he wanted to enter the cage to greet 600-pound Gilmore. The lion expert avowed that the big cat couldn't possibly remember him, but when Turner approached, Gilmore came over and licked him lovingly through the cage bars. Turner then entered the cage, with an associate that Gilmore also remembered. The visit was cordial until, as the associate stepped out of the cage, he saw the lion's mane rise ominously. Gilmore's glance became a glare as Turner turned toward the door: "You aren't thinking of leaving me again?"

Gilmore grabbed Turner and sank a canine dagger-tooth deep into his upper arm. Roscoe Turner instantly slammed the heel of his free hand into Gilmore's nose. The lion then released his old buddy, who nimbly exited the cage. The wound produced a serious infection, which for a time threatened Turner with amputation. Still, he occasionally revisited Gilmore, taking care to make a quick exit when his host didn't expect it.

More years passed as Roscoe Turner continued to support Gilmore, telling anyone who asked: "For a long time he paid my bills, now it's my turn to pay his." Gilmore died in 1952, at the grand old age of 22.

from CATS & KITTENS

Rebel, a Very Special Pony

KAREN BRAG

We met him on a cold, crisp December day. His owner was a college student desperate to find a home for him before Christmas vacation ended, and my four-year-old daughter was equally desperate to have her own pony. When we saw him, he was standing in a field looking at us. At least from the glow in his eyes when he tossed his thick mane, you could surmise he was looking at us. Dad got on him bareback, with just a halter and lead rope, and cantered across the pasture without getting bucked off, so we figured he'd be okay for Katie. That's how Rebel came into our lives.

Looking like a Welsh pony but without papers to prove it, Rebel was a short, stocky, furry bay gelding. Although, when we got him home and turned him out with our small band of Arabian mares, he promptly rounded them up and stood guard over them. He took his position of protector very seriously, running off the dogs and even the people that attempted to come near. Rebel, alias "Studly Doolittle," put on such an act that even our stallion, looking on from his private paddock, was a little disturbed. Rebel was immediately dispatched to his own private paddock, where more-gelding-like manners gradually returned.

Of course, Katie was never put off by his antics. He was just living up to his name. She discovered, in short order, that he loved peanut-butter-and-jam sandwiches and Oreo cookies. He discovered equally quickly when lunchtime was, and he waited at his fence by the backyard for the little blonde-headed girl with half her lunch in her hands. They became fast friends.

That spring we took Rebel trail riding. Our family spent nearly all of our vacations riding in the mountains, so we had to see what sort of trail horse he would be. On our first outing at Silver Falls State Park near Stayton, Oregon, we let Katie and Rebel lead down the trail so we could keep an eye on them. It soon became apparent that this was not such a good idea. Rebel had a strong dislike for larger horses. So strong was his dislike that he wouldn't wait to get crowded to kick. No, he would run backward up the trail to get his licks in! Rebel and Katie were relegated to the back of the line.

Katie, though, was content back there. She could hold Rebel back and canter to catch up. Soon they were jumping logs and practicing leads and learning to post at the trot. Rebel would go anywhere. He'd march through the brush around the windfalls and wade through the creeks like a pro. He carried Katie everywhere in the Central Oregon Cascade Mountains and Wilderness areas; Tam McArthur Rim, Green Lakes, Park Meadow, Sister's Mirror Lake. He made Katie a trail rider.

One spring day, a couple of years later, a group of us went riding at Silver Falls. We stopped at a wide intersection, tied up the horses, and sat down in the grass for lunch. The horses were all content and standing quietly, or so we thought. All of a sudden, there stood Rebel, his halter hanging on the tree where he had rubbed it off. Katie was frantic, but I calmly informed her that he wasn't about to go anywhere and leave all of the other horses. Boy, was I wrong. All he was lacking was a mustache to twist. He gave us an evil smile, complete with a glint in his eye, then turned and bolted down the trail, tail up over his back.

One of our group, Sarah, quickly mounted her horse and took off after Rebel. Katie was in tears, fearful she would never see him again. And I must admit, as we sat and waited for what seemed like hours, I began to have my doubts. Well, Sarah caught him, but not without running him down and literally forcing him off the trail into bushes he couldn't run through. We never tied him again without putting the halter on so tight it nearly strangled him.

Katie also had showring dreams, and Rebel seemed to know his stuff, so we gave that a try. I cautioned Katie about keeping him away from big horses because he might kick. Secretly, I crossed my fingers and hoped she could keep him from backing up into other exhibitors. I needn't have worried. He got to the show, took one look around, and became "Rebel the Show Horse."

He tucked his head, with reins hanging below his knees, and marched into that ring like he owned it. I could tell early on that he was paying attention to every word the announcer said (probably from the whiplash Katie got when gait changes were called for). His transitions were perfect. He never missed a cue—from the announcer, that is—and Katie sat there, smiling broadly, collecting ribbons. By the time she was seven, she was an experienced exhibitor, with a wall full of blue ribbons and shelves full of trophies.

As years passed, we found ourselves a bit crowded in the barn. We considered putting Rebel in the same paddock as our stallion, Sam. Now, Sam was known to be a bit of a coward.

During his own show career, his biggest problem was his lack of confidence when other horses crowded him. We weren't sure how he and Rebel would get along, but we thought we'd give it a try. Rebel promptly chased Sam out of his stall. Sam had never had to share his territory with anyone. He wasn't sure what to make of the little bay devil with the swishing tail and flattened ears. They had a delicate standoff for a while, then gradually Sam began to ask for his space back. Rebel acquiesced—to a point. They would share hay, but Sam got to keep his grain to himself. And when the weather was bad, they would *both* stand in the stall and watch it rain.

Rebel liked his new paddock. It was in front of the barn, bordering on both the driveway and the road. He soon learned Katie's bus schedule and would greet her daily with a whinny. She would reward him by saving her bread crusts and apple cores to feed him after school. On those occasional days when things weren't going right—a harsh word from me, an unfortunate comment by a friend at school—Katie would disappear to the barn with a handful of Oreos. The cookies were not for her. I don't know what she said to him; their conversations were very personal. I don't know what he said to her. All I know is when she came back to the house with cookie crumbs on her hands and horse "kisses" on her sleeves, she would be smiling and happy again.

For 10 years, Rebel and Katie belonged to each other. She developed confidence in rough backcountry and in showrings. While Rebel was still no angel and could cow-kick with the best of them, he was perfect with Katie. When no one else could make him move, she could pick up a canter from a standstill and change leads on the fly. On rainy afternoons when even Sam huddled in his stall, Rebel would wait up by the road for the bus and whinny when he saw it coming. Was it the apple cores and crusts of bread he waited for? I don't think so. I think it was Katie he wanted. And as for Katie, well, Rebel was just always there for her.

Old age is inevitable. It made its first impact on Rebel in the fall of 1989. Metabolic problems led to near-founder. His trail and show career ended but not his relationship to Katie. She looked after her old friend, hand-grazing him in the front yard, still taking her tears and smiles to share with him. I can't remember a morning he didn't whinny a greeting as she left for school or an afternoon he missed the arrival of her bus. She rode other horses on the trails and in the showrings, but Rebel still owned her heart.

Katie turned 14 this year. She is a long way from the 4-year-old with the long, golden pigtails flying down her back. This past year, she trained her own horse, a 3-year-old Arabian filly. As I watched her guide that youngster up the trail toward Green Lakes with tremendous confidence this summer, I thought about the first time she rode there on Rebel. As she calmly coaxed the 3-year-old over snowdrifts and across fast-flowing creeks, I silently thanked Rebel for all he had done. When she won her first blue ribbon on that frisky filly, I recalled that first blue Rebel had won for her. Was it luck we found him that December day? Or are some things just meant to be?

We said goodbye to Rebel on October 14, 1993. He will be missed.

from HEART SONGS FOR ANIMAL LOVERS

ACKNOWLEDGMENTS
(continued from page ii)

"The Language of Horses," by Monty Roberts, as told to Carol Kline, is from *Chicken Soup for the Pet Lover's Soul,* by Jack Canfield, Mark Victor Hansen, Marty Becker, D.V.M., and Carol Kline. © 1998 Jack Canfield, Mark Victor Hansen, Marty Becker and Carol Kline. Published by Health Communications, Inc.

"Bo's World," by Joe Kirkup, is condensed from *Northeast,* The Sunday Magazine of the *Hartford Courant,* May 14, 1995. The condensation appeared in *Reader's Digest,* June 1996.

"Murfee," "Which Way, Bruno?" and "A Special Investigator" are from *Everyday Heroes,* by Sherry Bennett Warshauer. Copyright © 1998 by Sherry Bennett Warshauer. Published by Howell Book House.

"Meet Flopsy" and "A Full Partner," by Donna Boetig, are from *McCall's,* February 1998.

"A Perfect Roommate," by Ed and Toni Eames, is from *Dog World,* September 1999.

"The Big Teddy Bear," by Sally Deneen, is from *Dog Fancy,* September 1999.

"Rare Gifts," by Christiane Lavin is from *Good Housekeeping,* August 1998.

"Feathered Friend," by Jo Coudert, appeared originally in *Reader's Digest,* May 1991. Copyright © 1991 by Jo Coudert.

"Requiem for a Junkyard Dog," by Dan Neil, is from *Car and Driver,* November 1998.

"Ebony, a Soldier" is from *Ebony and White,* by Joseph J. White. Copyright © 1996 by Doral Publishing, Inc. Published by Doral Publishing, Inc.

"Running Free," by Victoria Brehm, is from *Runner's World,* March 1994.

"Arson Dog on Duty," by Tim Simmons, is from *Dog Fancy,* February 1997.

"The Dog Nobody Wanted," by Collin Perry, is from *Reader's Digest,* December 1994.

"Be Careful—You Might Let Out a Bear" is from *It's a Jungle Out There,* by Gary Richmond. Copyright © 1996 by Harvest House Publishers. Published by Harvest House Publishers.

"Gilmore and Roscoe," by K. C. Tessendorf, is from *Cats & Kittens,* September 1999.

"Rebel, a Very Special Pony," by Karen Brag, is from *Heart Songs for Animal Lovers,* by Hester Mundis. Copyright © 1999 Hester Mundis. Published by Rodale Books.

A Note From the Editors

This original Guideposts series was created by the Book and Inspirational Media Division of the company that publishes *Guideposts,* a monthly magazine filled with true stories of people's adventures in faith. *Guideposts* is available by subscription. All you have to do is write to Guideposts, 39 Seminary Hill Road, Carmel, New York 10512. When you subscribe, each month you can count on receiving exciting new evidence of God's presence, His guidance and His limitless love for all of us.

Guideposts is also available on the Internet by accessing our home page on the World Wide Web at www.guideposts.org. Send prayer requests to our Monday morning Prayer Fellowship. Read stories from recent issues of our magazines, *Guideposts, Angels on Earth, Clarity, Guideposts for Kids* and *Guideposts for Teens,* and follow our popular book of daily devotionals, *Daily Guideposts.* Excerpts from some of our best-selling books are also available.